ARMORED ATTACK 1944

ARMORED ATTACK 1944

U.S. ARMY TANK COMBAT IN THE EUROPEAN THEATER FROM D-DAY TO THE BATTLE OF THE BULGE

Steven Zaloga

STACKPOLE
BOOKS

Published by
STACKPOLE BOOKS
5067 Ritter Road
Mechanicsburg, PA 17055
www.stackpolebooks.com

Printed in the United States of America

10 9 8 7 6 5 4 3 2 1

Library of Congress Cataloging-in-Publication Data

Zaloga, Steve.
    Armored attack 1944 : U.S. Army tank combat in the European theater from D-day to the Battle of the Bulge / Steven Zaloga.
        p. cm.
    Includes index.
    ISBN 978-0-8117-0769-5
    1. World War, 1939–1945—Tank warfare. 2. World War, 1939–1945—Tank warfare—Pictorial works. 3. World War, 1939–1945—Campaigns—Western Front. 4. World War, 1939–1945—Campaigns—Western Front—Pictorial works. 5. United States. Army—Armored troops—History. 6. United States. Army—Armored troops—History—Pictorial works. I. Title.
    D793.Z338 2011
    940.54'1273—dc22
                                                                2011005358

Contents

Introduction

THIS BOOK IS THE FIRST of a two-volume set covering U.S. Army armored units in combat in the European theater of operations from D-Day on 6 June 1944 through the end of the conflict in May 1945. The two volumes are split chronologically between 1944 and 1945. The aim of this book is to provide an in-depth visual record of armored combat through the eyes of the U.S. Army combat cameramen. Although the majority of the photos cover American armored vehicles, an extensive selection of photos of German vehicles is also included to help provide a more complete image of the fighting. However, the armored operations of Field Marshal Bernard Montgomery's neighboring British-Canadian 21st Army Group are outside the scope of this book. Nor does this book cover U.S. armored units in the Mediterranean theater of operations in Italy.

These photos come primarily from the main collection of World War II U.S. Army Signal Corps photos, which totals about a quarter of a million prints. This collection was initially housed at the Pentagon through the early 1970s when I first began to do my photo research. It was later transferred to the Defense Audio-Visual Agency facility at Bolling Air Force Base in Virginia and finally to the National Archives and Records Administration (NARA II) at College Park, Maryland, where it currently resides. The vast majority of the photos in this book come from this collection. A subsidiary Signal Corps collection resides at the U.S. Army Military History Institute at Carlisle Barracks, Pennsylvania, which also recently absorbed the rump Signal Corps collection held by the U.S. Army Center for Military History. In most cases, these photos duplicate the National Archives' holdings. Although the Signal Corps collections contain most of the surviving World War II photos, they do not contain all of them.

Many photos shot by Signal Corps combat cameramen were released through other venues during the war, such as the Office of War Information. A large portion of these photos are available at NARA II. In addition, other photos were never accepted into the main Signal Corps collection but were retained by separate organizations. For example, the library at the U.S. Military Academy at West Point has the Bradley Collection, which is a separate and distinct collection of Signal Corps photos, some of which are not located in the main Signal Corps holdings at the National Archives or Military History Institute. Finally, there are a variety of other smaller holdings at various archives, including the Patton Museum Library, formerly at Fort Knox, Kentucky, and the Ordnance Museum, formerly at Aberdeen Proving Ground. Besides the U.S. Army collections, there are also some useful photos of U.S. Army operations in the U.S. Navy and U.S. Air Force collections. It has taken me nearly forty years of research to collect the photos in this book.

The Signal Corps photos sometimes, but not always, include basic information on the date, location, and units depicted in the photo. This data is incomplete—and sometimes quite erroneous. Unit information is often lacking, and the spelling of the

European locations is notoriously erratic. For example, a series of photos identified as having been taken in Ploy, France, were actually taken in Parroy, France. Over the years, European military historians have done considerable work in more precisely identifying the actual location of these photos, and I have made every effort to try to correct this information when possible. However, a certain measure of uncertainty still remains about some of the details of many photos.

I have attempted to select the photos in this book to satisfy a variety of potential readers. I have included photos of interest to military historians covering significant battles. At the same time, I have attempted to include photos providing technical details that will appeal to military hobbyists such as military modelers, war-gamers, and historical reenactors. It is very difficult to achieve an ideal balance because of the very uneven coverage in wartime photos. After decades of research in the Signal Corps photos, I quickly discovered that combat photos taken during or shortly after major battles—such as Omaha Beach on D-Day or the first few days of fighting in the Ardennes in December 1944—are actually quite rare. Other events attracted a disproportionate amount of attention, so photo coverage of the liberation of Paris on 25 August 1944 was quite thorough. I have included some photos of poor technical quality as I believe these will be of interest to readers. Likewise, in the captions, I have tried to reach a balance between historical and technical information.

CHAPTER 1

Preparing for Overlord

THE FIRST CHAPTER OF THIS BOOK contains two main sections: a primer on the principal armored equipment of both sides during the 1944 fighting, followed by a survey of the preparations for D-Day, with an accent on training and specialized armored equipment.

Some basic description of U.S. Army organization is useful to help explain some of the unit designations that follow. American tank operations in the European theater of operations (ETO) involved two major types of formations, armored divisions and separate tank battalions. The armored divisions were intended primarily for mobile operations, and their chief role was to exploit deep behind enemy lines once a penetration had been won by the infantry. Of the sixteen armored divisions raised in World War II, all but one served in the ETO in 1944–45. (The 1st Armored Division served in the Mediterranean theater of operations in Italy in 1944–45). Armored divisions were a combined-arms force, and each had a balance of three tank battalions, three armored infantry battalions, and three armored field artillery battalions, plus supporting units. In total, they each contained 168 M4 medium tanks, 83 M5A1 light tanks, and a large number of other armored vehicles. The two exceptions to this organization were the 2nd and 3rd Armored Divisions, which retained the older 1942-pattern "heavy" organization, with six tank battalions instead of three, and so they had proportionately more equipment. Armored divisions in combat typically formed three combined-arms task forces, called combat commands for specific missions. These were designated as CCA, CCB, and CCR, the last being the divisional reserve. The component battalions in each of these combat commands varied from day to day so that units could be rotated out of combat for refit, replenishment, and rest.

The separate tank battalions were formed to provide support to the infantry. In France, most infantry divisions had a tank battalion and a tank destroyer attached to them for the conduct of specific operations. These tanks were used for close support of the infantry, and typically, one tank company would be attached to each of the infantry division's three infantry regiments. The equipment of these units was highly standardized, and nearly all units used the M4, M4A1, and M4A3 medium tank in their three medium tank companies and the M5A1 light tank in their single light tank company. The medium tanks were usually in Companies A, B, and C, while the light tanks were in Company D.

The separate tank destroyer battalions were formed and trained separately from the tank force, and their inspiration came mainly from the artillery branch. While the Armored Force was envisioned mainly as an offensive arm, the Tank Destroyer Command had been organized as a defensive response to the German *blitzkrieg*. U.S. Army infantry divisions were equipped with various antitank weapons, including the 2.36-inch "bazooka" rocket launcher and the towed 57mm antitank gun. Combat lessons from earlier in the war, however, suggested that these defenses could be overwhelmed when the Germans concentrated their panzers on a narrow front. The idea behind the tank destroyer force was that it could be kept in reserve until the main panzer attack materialized, and then the tank destroyer battalions could be rapidly sent to the point of greatest threat and overwhelm the panzer attack with fire and mobility. In practice, this doctrine proved to be seriously flawed, and instead, the tank destroyer battalions were usually doled out on a scale of one per infantry division and used much like the separate tank battalions.

Although the tank destroyer battalions initially relied on self-propelled guns as their principal equipment, the poor performance of these battalions in the North African theater led to a backwards step when many battalions were converted to towed 3-inch antitank guns in 1943–44. These towed gun battalions proved to be a failure in Normandy, and by 1945, the U.S. Army was in the process of shifting the tank destroyer battalions exclusively to self-propelled guns. The main self-propelled gun in these battalions was the M10 3-inch gun motor carriage (GMC), but the newer M18 76mm GMC and M36 90mm GMC were eventually deployed in the ETO as will be described in more detail below.

While tanks and tank destroyers were the backbone of American armored units in the ETO, there was a wide range of specialized infantry, artillery, and engineer vehicles; these are described in greater detail in the following pages.

AMERICAN ARMORED ARSENAL

The workhorse of the American tank force was the M4 medium tank. The British named it the General Sherman after the famous Civil War commander, but this name was not widely used by the U.S. Army during the war. This is a fairly typical mid-production M4 with the initial hull configuration but with the improved turret with the wider M34A1 gun mount that incorporated a new telescopic sight.

The stablemate of the M4 was the M4A1 medium tank. Both tanks were identical except that the M4 used a welded hull while the M4A1, as seen here, had a cast hull with much rounder contours. This tank from the 741st Tank Battalion on maneuvers in 1943 has the earlier turret configuration, which had the narrow M34 gun mount that relied on a less satisfactory periscopic gun sight. Most M4 and M4A1 tanks in Britain were subjected to a "quick fix" program in 1943 that incorporated a number of modifications, including the new M34A1 gun mount.

The U.S. Army began shifting to the improved M4A3 in the summer of 1944, substituting the Ford GAA inline engine for the Continental radial used in the earlier M4 and M4A1. This particular M4A3 also shows the new "wet stowage" hull, which shifted the ammunition out of the tank sponsons into the floor in protected racks to reduce the chances of dangerous ammunition fires if the tank was hit in combat. The first M4A3 tanks began appearing in the ETO in August–September 1944, but they did not become the predominant type until well into 1945.

The U.S. Army began shifting to a new 76mm gun on the Sherman family late in 1943. These first appeared on the M4A1(76mm), which, as seen here, also had a cast version of the wet ammo stowage hull with the larger driver hatches.

A special assault tank version of the Sherman was built in 1944, designated as the M4A3E2. It had substantially thicker armor than the normal version, which is most noticeable on its new turret. It was based on the M4A3 chassis but with thickened armor and was armed with the same 75mm gun as the usual version of the tank. It was intended for use in combat against fortified positions.

There was some controversy over the adoption of the 76mm gun because its high-explosive firepower was not as powerful as the older 75mm gun, even if its antitank performance was better. As a result, its combat debut was delayed until Operation Cobra at the end of July when contact with the German Panther tank convinced American tankers that a more powerful gun was needed.

The 76mm gun was also mounted on the preferred M4A3 chassis as the M4A3 (76mm). these first began to appear in the ETO after the M4A1(76mm), with their combat debut in August 1944 in small numbers. They did not become widespread until the autumn of 1944, and 75mm Shermans remained the majority until 1945.

To provide additional high-explosive fire support to the tank battalions, the 105mm howitzer was mounted in a modified M4 turret as the M4 (105mm) assault gun. The assault guns were used in tank battalion and company headquarters, mainly to provide indirect fire support for the line companies.

The final-production configuration of the 105mm assault gun was based on the M4A3 chassis with the new HVSS (horizontal volute suspension system). These began arriving in the final months of fighting in 1945.

The standard U.S. Army light tank in 1944 was the M5A1, known as the Stuart by the British. The standard-production version seen here had the exterior .30-caliber machine gun mounted on a simple pintle mount on the right side of the turret. There was generally one company of M5A1 light tanks in each tank battalion, compared to three companies of M4 medium tanks.

The most secret tank in U.S. Army service in the ETO was known only by code names such as Leaflet or T10 Shop Tractor. It was a night-fighting tank based on the British Canal Defence Light. It consisted of an M3A1 medium tank chassis with the normal turret replaced with a searchlight turret for nighttime target illumination. Six battalions of these were deployed to the ETO in 1944, but they were so secret that none of the field commanders was aware of their capabilities. Instead, they were converted to mine-exploder battalions. A few saw service in 1945 along the Rhine for night defense.

The final-production configuration of the M5A1 light tank had a folding .30-caliber machine-gun mount on the right side of the turret as seen here, with a sheet metal fairing over it. Other small improvements were also incorporated into M5A1 production in the summer of 1943, including a rear stowage bin on the hull.

The 37mm gun on the M5A1 was widely viewed as inadequate, and after a few attempts, the U.S. Army finally came up with a more acceptable design in 1944, the M24 light tank. It was armed with a lightweight 75mm gun with the same ballistic capabilities of the 75mm gun on the M4 medium tank, but its armor was much thinner. It began to reach the ETO late in 1944, and a handful saw service during the Ardennes fighting in 1944.

Like the M4 medium tank, there was an assault gun version of the M5A1 light tank, the M8 75mm howitzer motor carriage. This vehicle had an enlarged turret, which led to the deletion of the two front roof hatches. The 75mm howitzer was mounted in an open turret with a .50-caliber heavy machine-gun mount in the right rear corner for antiaircraft defense. These vehicles were widely used in armored cavalry units for fire support in 1944.

The M10 3-inch gun motor carriage saw continual evolutionary changes. The version here has the intermediate style of turret counterbalance at the rear of the turret.

U.S. Army doctrine favored a distinct armored vehicle to deal with enemy tanks: the tank destroyer. The principal type in the ETO was the M10 3-inch gun motor carriage (GMC). This consisted of an M4A2 medium tank chassis with a new superstructure and turret with a 3-inch (76mm) gun. The tank destroyers were more lightly armed than tanks, and the turret roof was completely open as seen in this overhead view.

By 1944, the gun on the M10 tank destroyer was not adequate to deal with improved German tanks like the Panther. As a result, a new turret was developed with a 90mm gun, which resulted in the M36 90mm gun motor carriage. These began to appear in the ETO in September–October 1944.

For industrial reasons, some M36 turrets were mounted on the normal M4A3 medium tank hull as the M36B1, and these also served in the ETO.

Tank destroyer doctrine favored speed over armor, and so the M10 3-inch gun motor carriage was regarded only as a stopgap until a faster tank destroyer arrived. This emerged as the M18 76mm gun motor carriage, which was armed with the same gun as the M4 (76mm) medium tanks, but on a light chassis. This was the fastest U.S. Army armored vehicle of the war, with a top road speed of 55 miles per hour, but the small chassis was tight and cramped compared to the M10, and speed proved to be less important in combat than in the dreams of tank destroyer advocates. As a result, the M18 was issued to only a small number of tank destroyer battalions in the ETO.

The U.S. Army used both light tanks and armored cars for reconnaissance in 1944. The principal type was the M8 light armored car, which had originally been designed as a wheeled tank destroyer armed with the standard 37mm antitank gun, but by the time it was ready, the gun was too small for the tank destroyer role. The armored cavalry was not happy about the lack of a heavy machine gun on the initial production series seen here, and most M8 armored cars in combat in the ETO had a ring mount for the .50-caliber heavy machine gun added above the turret.

A turretless version of the M8 light armored car was manufactured as the M20 armored utility vehicle. This was widely used as a headquarters and command vehicle and armed with a .50-caliber heavy machine gun on a ring mount over the open center compartment for self-defense.

High-explosive firepower in the American armored divisions was provided by armored self-propelled artillery in the form of the M7 105mm howitzer motor carriage. This consisted of the basic M4 medium tank chassis fitted with the standard 105mm howitzer. The .50-caliber machine gun in the "pulpit mount" prompted the British to call this vehicle the Priest.

This is an example of an intermediate-production M7 105mm howitzer motor carriage, manufactured in December 1942. It is fairly typical of the types seen in the ETO in the summer of 1944.

The final production series of the M7 105mm howitzer motor carriage in 1944 had many detail differences from the previous production batches. It has the heavy-duty vertical volute suspension with the one-piece return roller arms, late-style headlight and grouser box fittings, and the late-style rear sponson boxes with the basket on the top.

The U.S. Army's primary bunker-buster was the M12 155mm gun motor carriage, which mated a World War I French 155mm GPF gun on a medium tank chassis. These were deployed in separate artillery battalions, but they were often used in support of armored divisions during the fighting along the Siegfried Line in 1944, where their pointblank firepower was widely appreciated.

Since the M12 155mm gun motor carriage could carry very little ammunition on board, the special M30 cargo carrier was developed specifically to carry its ammunition.

The armored infantry relied on half-tracks for transport. Two basic types of half-track were in use in 1944: the M2 half-track armored car and the M3 half-track. The M2 half-track car had a shorter superstructure and was fitted with large stowage bins in the middle of the compartment for stowage, as can be seen here with the side access door open. This vehicle was intended to act as a prime mover for towed guns and as a scout vehicle.

This overhead view of the M2 half-track car shows the smaller space of the interior compartment because of the two large stowage bins behind the driver.

As can be seen in this rear overhead shot of an M2 half-track car, the stowage bins filled up a considerable portion of the hull interior behind the driver.

This overhead view of an M3 half-track shows the larger and more spacious rear compartment. This was the predominant version of the half-track family in the ETO in 1944–45.

This rear overhead image of a M3 half-track shows the more spacious accommodations in the rear body compared to the M2 half-track car.

The M3 half-track was the personnel-carrier version of the half-track family and was intended primarily to carry armored infantry units.

The final production series of the M2 and M3 half-tracks introduced a ring mount for a .50-caliber heavy machine gun above the right seat. These versions were designated as M2A1 and M3A1, the latter of which is shown here.

To provide fire support for the armored infantry battalion, a special mortar-carrier version of the half-track was designed, the M4 81mm mortar motor carriage. It was based on the M2 half-track car and had the mortar facing rearward. This configuration was not entirely popular, and many units modified the mortar to fire forward.

The M15A1 combination gun motor carriage was the other major antiaircraft version of the half-track in the ETO. The boxy rear turret contained a 37mm automatic cannon and two .50-caliber heavy machine guns. Each armored division deployed an antiaircraft artillery weapons company consisting of eight M16 machine-gun motor carriages and eight M15A1 combination gun motor carriages.

Antiaircraft defense of the armored divisions was provided in part by the M16 machine-gun motor carriage, which consisted of a power-operated Maxson turret in the rear bed of a modified M3 half-track with four .50-caliber heavy machine guns. An expedient version of the M16 was also used in the ETO by taking towed Maxson turrets and mounting them in surplus M2 half-tracks—sometimes called a "Patterson conversion" after their inventor.

A variety of specialized armored vehicles was deployed to support tank units. Among the most important were the tank-recovery vehicles. The standard tank-recovery vehicle early in the war was the T2, later designated as the M31 tank-recovery vehicle. This was an M3 medium tank with its armament removed and a special crane fitted to the turret.

This shows how the Gar Wood 10-Y 5500 crane was deployed on the T2 (M31) for hoisting. This was often used for extracting engines from M4 medium tanks and similar tasks. This particular example is based on an M3A3 hull.

The U.S. Army switched to tank-recovery vehicles based on the M4 medium tank family in 1944 as the M32 tank-recovery vehicle. These used a completely new turret as seen in this overhead view of an M32B2 (T5E2) based on the M4A2 chassis. Other versions were based on other models of the M4; for example, the M32 tank-recovery vehicle was based on the M4, the M32B1 on the M4A1, and so on.

Another specialized application of the M4 medium tank for engineering missions was the flail tank, which was designed to explode enemy mines. The added framework contained a motor that rotated a flail drum with heavy chains to detonate mines on impact. The T3 Scorpion mine exploder was based on the British Scorpion, though it differed in a number of technical details. It was used in Italy in 1943–44 and, in small numbers, in southern France in the summer of 1944. It was not especially effective, and the U.S. Army in the ETO obtained some of the later British Sherman Crab flail tanks instead.

Another approach to dealing with the mine threat was a set of heavy wheels that could withstand mine blasts. The T1E3 mine exploder was named Aunt Jemima after the popular pancake brand. Although fairly effective on dry ground, this type of mine exploder was apt to become bogged down in soft or wet soil.

The U.S. Army adopted specialized high-speed tractors based on tank components for the mechanization of the field artillery. The M4 high-speed tractor was used to tow the 155mm gun, 8-inch howitzer, and 90mm antiaircraft gun.

The smaller M5 high-speed tractor was used primarily to tow the 155mm howitzer. Both the M4 and M5 high-speed tractors had compartments in the rear of the vehicle for carrying ammunition for the guns that they towed.

GERMAN PANZER ARSENAL

The backbone of the German panzer force was the Panzerkampfwagen IV (Pz.Kpfw. IV), which made up more than half of the tank inventory in France in 1944. It was roughly equivalent to the M4 Sherman.

A Pz.Kpfw. IV Ausführung H ("Type H") captured in Normandy by the Allies with Allied white stars hastily painted on. The later versions of the Pz.Kpfw. IV had *Schürzen* ("skirts") attached to the turret and hull sides; in this view, the side skirts are missing. Although these are often described as defenses against bazookas, in fact they were fielded on the Russian front in 1943 as a defense against the ubiquitous Soviet antitank rifles that could otherwise penetrate the thin side armor of German tanks at close range.

The most powerful opponent of the M4 Sherman in Normandy was the Pz.Kpfw. V, better known as the Panther. It had superior firepower, armor, and mobility to the M4 tank. It was first encountered by American forces in mid-July 1944 during the fighting with the Panzer Lehr Division along the Vire River. Seen here is the most common version in the summer of 1944, the Panther Ausf. A.

The Panther underwent continual evolution, and by the autumn of 1944, the most common version encountered by U.S. troops was the Panther Ausf. G, which had a simplified hull with a single-piece side plate. This particular Panther Ausf. G is one of the rare variants fitted with steel-rimmed road wheels.

Although most American accounts of tank fighting make reference to encounters with Tiger tanks, the U.S. Army seldom, if ever, encountered the Tiger I in combat in the ETO in 1944. There were few Tiger units in Normandy, and they were in the British and Canadian sectors.

While encounters with the Tiger tank were infrequent, American forces did engage its larger successor, the King Tiger, starting in August 1944. The first combat encounters with the King Tiger occurred in the fighting in the Mantes bridgehead on the Seine River north of Paris. This example was captured in the Ardennes in 1944 and is seen on display after the war at Aberdeen Proving Ground, Maryland, next to a Red Army KV-1 heavy tank.

One of the most widely encountered German armored vehicles in 1944 was the Sturmgeschütz III (StuG III) assault gun. This consisted of the Pz.Kpfw. III chassis with a fixed casemate and a long 75mm gun. These were primarily used by the assault-gun companies of the infantry divisions, which nominally had fourteen of these. They were used both for direct-fire support of the infantry as well as antitank defense.

The most potent of the German tank destroyers was the Jagdpanzer IV/70, sometimes called "Guderian's Duck" after the famous German panzer commander. This was the Pz.Kpfw. IV chassis fitted with a fixed superstructure and the excellent 75mm gun used on the Panther tank. Although this vehicle had the frontal armor and firepower of the Panther, it was tactically less flexible because of the lack of the turret and was prone to mishaps because of the awkward mounting of the long gun tube.

German infantry divisions nominally had an assault-gun company with StuG III and another Panzerjäger (tank destroyer) company with various types of vehicles. One of the more common types of Panzerjäger encountered in Normandy was the Marder III, which consisted of the 75mm PaK 40 antitank gun mounted on the chassis of the obsolete Czechoslovakian Pz.Kpfw. 38(t) light tank. Although too lightly armored for a tank duel, these weapons were quite deadly when used from ambush and could easily penetrate the Sherman's armor. This Panzerjäger 38(t) Ausf. M Marder III of Panzerjäger Abteilung 61 of the 11th Panzer Division was knocked out in the fighting with the U.S. 6th Armored Division on 22 November 1944 near St. Jean Rohrbach.

The most effective German tank destroyer was the Jagdpanther, combining the long 88mm gun of the King Tiger on the Panther tank chassis. These were rarely encountered by the U.S. Army in 1944 until the Ardennes fighting in December 1944. They were deployed in special heavy tank destroyer battalions, not in divisional antitank companies.

The Jagdpanzer 38(t), sometimes called the Hetzer, is mistaken for a tank hunter because of its designation. In fact, it was deployed most often as a low-cost alternative to the StuG III in the assault-gun role. Although sleek and modern looking, it was lightly armored and very cramped. It was not encountered in large numbers by the U.S. Army until late in 1944.

The Sd.Kfz. 250 light half-track was roughly the equivalent of the U.S. Army's M2 half-track car. It was significantly smaller than the Sd.Kfz. 251 and intended for use in reconnaissance units and a variety of other specialized tasks.

The German equivalent of the U.S. Army's M3 half-track was the Sonder-kraftfahrzeuge (Sd.Kfz.) 251 medium half-track. This was used as an armored infantry carrier and also served as the basis for a variety of specialized subvariants.

While much of the attention on tank losses focuses on enemy tanks, the Sherman's most dangerous adversary was probably the 75mm PaK 40, the standard German antitank gun in 1944, which was widely deployed in infantry and panzer divisions. Not only could it penetrate the Sherman from any angle, but its small size made it easy to conceal and ideal for ambush. While American accounts repeatedly speak about receiving 88mm fire, 88mm guns were exceedingly rare, and on most occasions, the fire was coming from one of the ubiquitous PaK 40.

The German army used a variety of armored cars, of which the best was the Sd.Kfz. 234/2 Puma. It was armed with a 50mm gun and had a very advanced suspension. It was built in several other versions with different armament, but none of the type was widely encountered by the U.S. Army in 1944.

Although the 88mm flak gun was a legendary tank killer, it was not a particularly common opponent of American tanks in 1944. These weapons were quite expensive, cumbersome to deploy, and vulnerable to fire. Although sometimes used in an antitank role, more often than not they were used in their intended role in rear areas for antiaircraft defense.

The best German antitank gun in service in 1944 was the 88mm PaK 43. Unlike the 88mm flak gun, these were specifically designed for tank fighting with a carriage optimized for quick deployment. Although very powerful, they were not particularly common and were issued to special corps-level, not divisional, antitank units. This captured example is seen here being used by American troops for field artillery until captured ammunition stocks were exhausted.

The Panzerschreck ("tank terror") was a crew-served antitank rocket launcher that was more accurate than the Panzerfaust at longer ranges. Inspired by the U.S. Army's 2.36-inch bazooka, it was larger and used an 88mm rocket projectile. Here, a Panzerschreck is compared to a bazooka in front of a Tiger tank captured in Tunisia in 1943.

The advent of cheap antitank rockets made the 1944 battlefield much deadlier for tanks. The Panzerfaust ("tank fist") was a disposable rocket-powered antitank projectile that was very deadly when used properly, but effective only from short ranges.

TRAINING IN BRITAIN

American tank units first began to arrive in Britain in 1942. This is an exercise on Perham Downs by an M3 medium tank battalion in December 1942. The M3 medium tank, known by the British as the General Lee, was obsolete by the time of D-Day and was replaced by the M4 medium tank series before D-Day.

U.S. tank units continued their training in England in the months leading up to D-Day. This M5A1 light tank taking part in war games has white crosses applied in temporary paint to mark it as a member of the "opposing forces."

An M5 light tank of the 102nd Cavalry during training at Chiseldon Camp in 1943. This particular version of the Stuart tank was largely replaced by 1944 with the M5A1 version, which had an improved turret with a rear bustle to accommodate the tank radio.

An M2 half-track of the 827th Engineer Aviation Battalion on training in England on 26 March 1943. This was one of a number of segregated African-American engineer units that served in the ETO.

Engineers in England experiment with ways to float an M2A1 half-track across a stream using inflatable pontoons in April 1943.

Besides its extensive training efforts in England, the U.S. Army also helped raise and equip the French First Army, which was deployed in August 1944 in southern France as part of Operation Dragoon. This is a pre-invasion training exercise by an M4A4 medium tank and M8 75mm howitzer motor carriage. The French First Army's 1st and 5th Armored Divisions used the Napoleonic regimental banner on the hull sides as their distinctive marking. These units were raised and trained primarily in French North Africa.

Eisenhower and Montgomery paid a visit to the 3rd Armored Division during training at Warminister, England, on February 25, 1944. SHAEF deputy commander Arthur Tedder is immediately behind Ike, and to the left is Maj. Gen. Leroy Watson, the divisional commander.

To help prepare troops for the D-Day amphibious landings, the U.S. Army set up a number of coastal exercise sites. Among these was the U.S. Assault Training Center located around the village of Woolacombe in Devon on the western coast of England. This is a tank-training exercise with an M4 tank being delivered by an LCM (landing craft, mechanized) on 23 October 1943.

Here, the M4 has cleared the ramp of the LCM. This provides a good look at the two wading trunks that were used to prevent the engine from being flooded if the tank was dropped in shallow water. The tank could "deep wade" in water up to the top of its turret if necessary.

A trio of M4 medium tanks leaves the beach at the U.S. Assault Training Center during the 23 October 1943 exercise.

Another view of the 23 October 1943 exercise. Although the LCM was commonly used in the early exercises, this landing option was rejected for use on D-Day because of the limited capacity of the LCM to operate in the English Channel due to the weight of the M4 tank.

A close-up of one of the M4 medium tanks at the U.S. Assault Training Center.

A pair of M4 tanks fitted with wading trunks engaging in firing exercises along the English coast in 1944. The hills over the beaches closely resemble the terrain conditions at Omaha Beach. The U.S. Army also made extensive use of training facilities at Slapton Sands in England.

An exercise involving an LCT (landing craft, tank) with five M3 medium tanks as its cargo. Although these training exercises often used the small LCMs, plans for the Overlord invasion anticipated the use of the much larger LCTs because of the conditions in the English Channel and the marginal capabilities of the LCM with a load as heavy as a tank.

Deep-wading trunks were first developed by the Fifth Army Invasion Training Center (5AITC) in Algeria in 1943 for the Operation Husky landings on Sicily in July 1943. The design was refined, and this shows the standardized deep-wading trunks manufactured in the U.S. Besides fitting the trunks to the tank, extensive waterproofing had to be done to each tank to prevent water from leaking inside.

An M5A1 light tank prepared for deep wading. The tank battalions used in the assault waves on D-Day did not deploy their light tank companies during the initial assault, but the light tanks had to be waterproofed for their eventual landing.

A rear view of an M5A1 light tank with the standard deep-wading kit fitted.

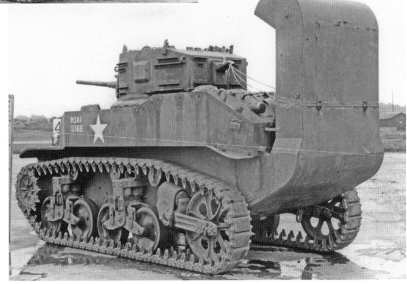

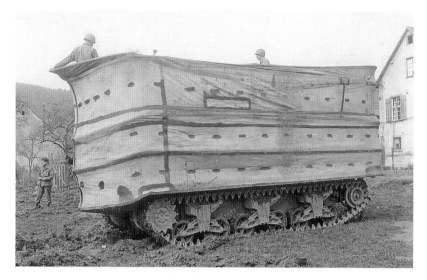

The most controversial tank used on D-Day was the Duplex-Drive Sherman, also known as the DD or Donald Duck tank. This British invention consisted of a canvas screen erected by pneumatic tubes inside the screen to provide buoyancy and a pair of propellers in the rear driven off the drive sprockets. These tanks were so secret that few photos were taken prior to D-Day. This photo shows a DD tank during the Rhine operations in 1945.

The DD tank screen gave the Sherman reasonable buoyancy when the tank was empty as seen here during training, but when fully loaded, there was far less freeboard.

Once the DD tank landed, the air was drained from the pressure tubes inside the canvas skirt, which collapsed the skirt down to allow the gun to be used. This is a training exercise in 1945. A total of 350 of these M4A1 tanks were converted in the United States in 1944 for use in the D-Day operation by American, British, and Canadian units.

The original U.S. Army scheme to deal with German antitank fortifications in Normandy was to demolish them with the Mark 5 "Cowcatcher" 7.2-inch rocket launcher. While the 7.2-inch rockets proved to be quite effective against concrete, the awkward location of the launcher was quickly rejected in favor of a launcher mounted over the roof.

To deal with the German coastal bunkers and antitank walls on the D-Day beaches, the U.S. Army planned to use the engineer armored vehicle armed with an overhead Mark 6 (T2) rocket launcher instead of the British Churchill AVRE (Armoured Vehicle Royal Engineers) armed with a Petard spigot mortar. Because of delays in the engineer armored vehicle program, the U.S. Army decided instead to use the demolition rocket launcher on normal M4 tanks in the separate tank battalions rather than in dedicated engineer units.

The T40 Whiz-Bang demolition rocket launcher fired 7.2-inch high-explosive rockets. Here, at trials at Fort Knox, is one of the prototypes mounted on a M4A2 medium tank.

This rear view provides details of the T40 Whiz-Bang launcher on an M4A2 pilot. The launcher had twenty launch cells, and the rockets could be fired singly or ripple fired. As can be seen, the clearance between the launcher rack and the turret roof made it impossible to use the turret hatches, and this caused so much concern from the crews that the project was abandoned shortly before D-Day, even after some M4 tanks of the 70th Tank Battalion had been fitted with the launcher.

Another way to deal with German bunkers on the Normandy beaches was the flamethrower tank. The U.S. ordered fifty Sherman Crocodiles from Britain in February 1944, but none was delivered until after the invasion. The Sherman Crocodile used the same fuel trailer as the original Churchill Crocodile, but had a small turreted flamethrower added on the right front hull corner. This is the pilot during trials.

To deal with the threat of mines on the invasion beaches, a number of mine-exploding devices were tested. This is a demonstration of two T1E3 mine exploders in England in May 1944 to familiarize armored units with its capability.

This demonstration in England in May 1944 before D-Day illustrates the limitations of using the T1E3 Aunt Jemima on soft sand beaches. As a result of this and other trials, the U.S. Army decided against using mine-clearing tanks on D-Day. However, the T1E3 mine exploders were later used in the campaigns along the German frontier in the autumn of 1944.

The most useful engineer tank deployed on D-Day was the dozer tank, which was a normal Sherman fitted with a bulldozer blade. To help destroy German antitank walls, these vehicles were supposed to carry a large high-explosive pack on the front of their blades which could be deposited at the base of the wall before being detonated. The units viewed this idea as far too dangerous, and it was not widely used on D-Day. Instead, the dozer tanks were used mainly to clear obstructions with their blades.

One of the more peculiar mistakes in D-Day planning was the failure to use the LVT amphibious tractors to assist in the initial landing waves. These had proven to be invaluable in the Pacific campaign starting at Tarawa in 1943. There were 300 of these LVTs available in England, and this is a view of a park containing LVT-1 and LVT-2 amtracs in England in March 1944. A handful of LVTs participated in the D-Day landings to carry supplies, but the vast majority remained in England.

A rare glimpse of one of the ultra-secret Leaflet tanks of the 736th Tank Battalion (Special) on an M26 Dragon Wagon in England prior to D-Day, based on the cast-hull M3A1 medium tank.

A close-up of the turret of a Leaflet tank of the 736th Tank Battalion (Special) in England prior to D-Day. The American version of the Canal Defence Light had several differences from the British version, including the use of a Browning .30-caliber machine gun in the turret next to the searchlight aperture.

The 2nd Armored Division during its training operations in England made some changes to its half-tracks. With the arrival of new M10 3-inch tank destroyers, the 41st Armored Infantry took the 37mm gun mountings off the retired M6 gun motor carriages and mounted them onto an M2 half-track car to provide them with added firepower. This photo was taken in England in April 1944 before the Normandy landings.

Another innovation by the 41st Armored Infantry was a rearrangement of the M4 mortar motor carriage. These vehicles normally had the 81mm mortar pointed over the rear of the vehicle. In the 2nd Armored Division, this was reversed, and the mortar pointed forward, which the unit felt was a more useful configuration.

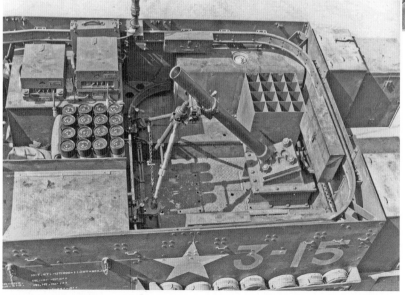

A close-up view of the interior of the M4 mortar motor carriage of 41st Armored Infantry showing the revised interior layout. The original configuration with the rear-facing mortar resulted from concern over the muzzle blast of the mortar, but the troops preferred the convenience of a forward-facing mortar since the half-track could be brought into action more quickly in this revised configuration.

A column of M2A1 half-tracks of the 18th Infantry, 1st Infantry Division, on exercise in Devonshire on 7 May. Some units kept the old weapons to supplement divisional firepower. The 1st Infantry Division landed on Omaha Beach on D-Day.

A group of M4 tanks of the 6th Armored Division on exercise on the Salisbury plains prior to D-Day. The nearest tank, named *Assam Dragon*, is fitted with a large reel of field telephone wire, an occasional modification conducted in the United Kingdom, mainly on headquarter tanks.

A column of M26 Dragon Wagon tank transporters moves vehicles near Bristol on 20 March. The M15A1 semi-trailer used with the M26 tractor was designed to accommodate an M4 medium tank, but as seen here, it is carrying two M5A1 light tanks.

An M10 3-inch gun motor carriage sets off for exercises in England in March. The M10 was the standard U.S. Army tank destroyer in 1944.

An M10 3-inch gun motor carriage (named *Bouncing TNT*) and its crew from Company B, 803rd Tank Destroyer Battalion, 2nd Armored Division, in Cornwall, England, in April. This unit has added a set of large pipes on the four corners of the hull, presumably intended to support camouflage nets. This provides a good example of full official stowage patterns, including the tripod for the .50-caliber machine gun on the hull side and the turret rain tarp on the turret roof forward of the opening.

A view from above the turret of an M10 tank destroyer looking toward the turret floor during crew training while the commander explains the use of the breech block crank held in his right hand. Unlike the Sherman, the turret roof of the tank destroyers was completely open since they were not intended to be used for close combat against enemy infantry.

An M15A1 combination gun motor carriage of the 474th Anti-Aircraft Artillery Battalion takes part in a practice landing at Slapton Sands in England on 27 April during the D-Day preparations. The M15A1 antiaircraft vehicle was armed with a 37mm cannon flanked on either side by .50-caliber heavy machine guns. Slapton Sands was the scene of a major disaster during the preparations for the Normandy landing when some German torpedo boats torpedoed a troop ship taking part in landing exercises in the predawn hours of 28 April. The 474th landed at Normandy on D-Day.

The M18 76mm gun motor carriage was a new tank destroyer on a newer and faster chassis than the old M10 tank destroyer. This is the 603rd Tank Destroyer Battalion of the 6th Armored Division training in England in May. This was one of the first M18 battalions committed to combat in July during Operation Cobra.

A pair of M10 3-inch gun motor carriages comes ashore during training exercises in Britain prior to the D-Day landings, with an LCT and LST in the background.

The other antiaircraft half-track used by the U.S. Army in 1944 was the M16, which was armed with four .50-caliber heavy machine guns in a power-operated Maxson turret. This M16 is seen coming ashore off an LCT during training exercises in England on 6 May.

An panoramic view of an armored regiment of the 2nd Armored Division at their staging location in southern England in May prior to the Normandy invasion. As can be seen to the lower right, several of the M4 medium tanks have already been fitted with wading trunks.

An M29 Weasel tracked utility vehicle named *Snookie* is prepared for loading at a British port prior to the D-Day landings in Normandy. These small tracked vehicles were widely used in engineer units in the Normandy campaign.

A number of M29 Weasels and jeeps congregate on a dock in England prior to being embarked on an LST for D-Day.

M4 high-speed tractors towing 90mm antiaircraft guns move their vehicles into an LST (landing ship, tank) in southern England in the build-up prior to D-Day.

A battery of 155mm howitzers towed by M5 high-speed tractors of a field artillery battalion prepares to load aboard landing ships at a port in southern England prior to the D-Day landings.

The M4 high-speed tractors of the 110th Anti-Aircraft Artillery Gun Battalion (Mobile) move its weapons into the hold of LST-506 prior to embarking to Normandy.

A final view of the preparations of the 110th Anti-Aircraft Artillery Gun Battalion (Mobile) during embarkation in England. This battalion landed in France on D+1, 7 June.

An M4 fitted with deep-wading trunks is loaded aboard a transport ship in Britain in June.

An M16 antiaircraft half-track (named *Der Fuehrer's Express*) loads onto an LST in Portsmouth Harbor on 1 June 1944.

The crew of an M4 medium tank prepares to load its tank at a port in southern England prior to the D-Day landings.

A line-up of M7 105mm howitzer motor carriages of Battery B, 14th Armored Field Artillery Battalion, 2nd Armored Division, already waterproofed and ready to be shipped to France. The 2nd Armored Division added stowage racks on the hull side, like those on half-tracks.

The D-Day plans intended to land towed 105mm howitzers for fire support of the infantry regiments using DUKW amphibious trucks as seen here. However, most foundered at sea after the crews had overburdened the vehicles with sand bags and extra ammunition, not anticipating the rough seas off Normandy.

An M7 105mm howitzer motor carriage (named *Big Chief III*) of Battery B, 42nd Armored Field Artillery Battalion, is prepared for the D-Day landings at Portsmouth on 1 June. The vehicle has had a fording screen erected around the fighting compartment and a set of wading trunks fitted at the rear to enable it to be driven to shore through the surf to a depth of about ten feet.

An M7 105mm howitzer motor carriage crew prepares for loading onto an LCT in an English harbor in June. Canvas wading skirts have been fitted around the gun to prevent flooding the fighting compartment. The front of the hull is stowed with the usual kit, including a large artillery camouflage net on the right fender.

A captain signals another M7 105mm howitzer motor carriage while loading an LCT in Britain prior to the D-Day landings. The howitzer motor carriages are fitted for deep wading, and both have large camouflage nets rolled up and stowed on their bows.

A number of M7 105mm howitzer motor carriages on an LCT in an English harbor prior to D-Day. This shows the extensive waterproofing on the vehicles prior to debarkation, including wading stacks for the engine and a wading curtain around the fighting compartment to minimize flooding.

Troops in England prepare their M3A1 half-track for D-Day. The tube seen on the far left is a wading tube connected to the engine to feed air in the event that the half-track was partially submerged when wading ashore. The large Allied star marking on the hood has the hollow sections painted in gas-detection paint, which changed color from green to orange in the presence of chemical agents. There was still considerable concern before D-Day that the Germans would use chemical warfare in their defense of Normandy.

An LCT loads at a port in Devonshire on the southern English coast on 4 June 1944 prior to the Normandy landings. This LCT is carrying M4 tanks of the 70th Tank Battalion, and one of the unit's T2 tank recovery vehicles is backing up the access ramp at the front. These vehicles are fitted with deep-wading trunks, and they were landed on D-Day at Utah Beach.

CHAPTER 2

D-Day: The Overlord Invasion

THE LANDINGS IN NORMANDY on D-Day included the use of a separate tank battalion to support each of the three assault regiments. So at Omaha Beach, two tank battalions were the first units scheduled to land, and at Utah, another tank battalion provided fire support to the initial waves of troops. These battalions were deployed with two companies of M4 Duplex Drive (DD, nicknamed "Donald Duck") amphibious tanks and one company of M4s with deep-wading trunks. Because of the fragility of the DD tanks in rough seas, the army and navy reached a last-minute understanding that in the event of strong waves, the navy's LCTs (landing craft, tank) would bring the DD tanks all the way to Omaha Beach instead of launching them from the daunting range of 5,000 yards off shore.

In the case of the 741st Tank Battalion, which was landing in support of the 16th Infantry of the 1st Infantry Division near the Colleville draw, the over-eager army tank captains overruled the advice of the navy skippers and launched their two DD tank companies at sea. Of the twenty-nine tanks that launched, twenty-seven sank and only two reached shore; three more were landed on the beach by the LCT. After the battalion's company of deep-wading tanks landed safely, this sector of the beach had only

sixteen of its intended fifty-six tanks. The neighboring 743rd Tank Battalion, supporting the 116th Infantry of the 29th Division, landed near the Vierville draw in much better condition. The commander of the LCT flotilla convinced the two DD tank company commanders to land on shore from the LCTs, and as a result, twenty-eight DD tanks were landed safely. Nearly all of the deep-wading M4 tanks landed safely, except for those lost to enemy action, so this sector had forty-two of its intended fifty-six tanks.

In spite of the heavy losses suffered during landings, the tanks began to provide immediate assistance to the beleaguered infantry that had quickly followed them ashore. The Germans had reinforced Omaha Beach with numerous steel-reinforced concrete pillboxes that were nearly impervious to naval gunfire since their embrasures pointed along the shore, not facing the sea. Two of these were armed with the powerful 88mm PaK 41/43 antitank gun, giving the beach garrison the concrete equivalent of a King Tiger tank at either end of the beach. There were numerous other bunkers with 50mm and 75mm guns—essentially concrete panzers that could be knocked out only by a direct hit into their small embrasures. The American tanks spent most of the day trying to eliminate these bunkers and other defenses. The commander of the 2nd Battalion, 116th Infantry, later said that the tanks had "saved the day. They shot the hell out of the Germans and got the hell shot out of them." Of the fifty-eight tanks successfully landed at the start of D-Day, forty-two were still in action at the end of the day, mostly in the Vierville draw area with the 743rd Tank Battalion.

In contrast to Omaha, the landings at Utah Beach proved much less costly. The 70th Tank Battalion launched twenty-eight DD tanks at varying ranges to the beach, and only one sank. The deep-wading tanks were also successful, and the tanks proved instrumental in leading the 4th Infantry Division over the causeways to link up with the paratroopers who had landed farther inland the night before. For these three tank battalions, it was only the start of a very long campaign. The 70th Tank Battalion was the longest-serving American tank battalion, having previously fought in the North African and Sicily campaigns.

An M4 dozer tank and an M4A1 with M8 ammo trailer named *Aide de Camp* of Company A, 741st Tank Battalion, on board the LCT set off for Omaha Beach from Britain. This battalion landed on the eastern side of Omaha on D-Day in support of the 16th Infantry, 1st Infantry Division.

A photo of Omaha Beach on D-Day afternoon showing a considerable amount of debris in the water as well as the congestion in the beach approaches.

The most imposing antitank defenses on the Normandy beaches were the powerful 88mm PaK 43/41 antitank guns, the towed version of the gun on the Tiger tank. On Omaha, there were two of these weapons on the eastern and western ends, able to cover the entire landing zone thanks to their long range. This one was in a Regelbau 677 (construction standard; Rgl. Nr.) bunker in the WN61 strongpoint on the eastern side of the Colleville draw on Beach Fox Green. Its crew was killed by a direct hit from a Sherman DD tank of the 741st Tank Battalion early in the morning. Late in the day, this gun was pulled out of the bunker so that the structure could be used as a protected medical post.

The Rgl. Nr. 677 88mm gun bunker in strongpoint WN61 in the Colleville draw is seen here late on D-Day after being converted to a medical aid station. Its gun embrasure was covered over by a canvas tarp. This was the most powerful weapon in Strongpoint Colleville, but it ultimately played the least significant role in the fighting because of its early destruction by tank fire.

The other side of the Colleville draw contained strongpoint WN62, which was bristling with weapons. This is a camouflaged gun pit containing a pedestal-mounted 50mm antitank gun.

The WN62 strongpoint on "Engineer Hill" contained two gun bunkers armed with these World War I–vintage 76.5mm FK M17 field guns. These engaged in running gun duels with American tanks and naval destroyers for much of the morning, with the bunkers taking dozens of hits. This is the view alongside one of the bunkers after the field gun had been pulled outside to make use of the bunker as an aid station.

One of the more curious German defenses on Omaha Beach was the Goliath remote-control demolition tank. These little vehicles carried an explosive charge and were intended to serve as robotic mines that could be steered into tanks or landing craft. However, they arrived only days before the Allied landing, and their wire guidance proved to be fragile.

Although of poor quality, this is a rare image of one of the few DD tanks of the 741st Tank Battalion that reached the beach in the Colleville sector. Of the battalion's thirty-two DD tanks, all but five sank, and of these, three were quickly knocked out by German guns in the WN61 and WN62 resistance nests.

A deep-wading M4 of Company A, 741st Tank Battalion, is seen here on Omaha after it bogged down in the soft sand beyond the German beach obstructions.

This is *Adeline II*, an M4A1 tank of Company A, 741st Tank Battalion, damaged on Omaha Beach on D-Day. *Adeline*'s rear bogie assembly was hit by a 50mm antitank gun during a duel with a German bunker to the west of the WN62 resistance nest. The damaged bogie prevented it from moving over the sea wall. It is seen here on 7 June being towed through the village of Colleville-sur-Mer by one of the battalion's M31 tank-recovery vehicles.

Another view of *Adeline II* being recovered on D+1. This is one of the few clear photos to have survived of the tanks of the 741st Tank Battalion on Omaha.

The most common antitank guns on the Normandy beaches were old German 50mm tank and antitank guns that had been converted into pedestal-mounted weapons. This is one of the concrete gun pits east of the Colleville draw with large amounts of expended ammunition littering the site.

Strongpoint St. Laurent in the middle of Omaha Beach was still under construction on D-Day, with many of its bunkers incomplete. This is an overhead view of the Les Moulin draw on D-Day, the dividing line between Dog Red and Easy Green Beaches. The numerous tanks seen in this view are mostly from the 743rd Tank Battalion, which landed on the western side of Omaha in support of the 116th Infantry, 29th Division.

The most famous bunker in resistance nest WN65 in the E-1 St. Laurent draw was this Rgl. Nr. 667 armed with a 50mm pedestal gun. It caused considerable havoc on D-Day before being knocked out by concerted fire from M15A1 antiaircraft half-tracks of the 467th Anti-Aircraft Artillery Battalion.

The embrasure of the 50mm pedestal gun bunker in WN65. These bunkers were positioned with the embrasures facing along the beach, with their heaviest concrete protection toward the sea to protect them from naval gunfire.

This is a view from inside the WN65 50mm bunker, with considerable damage evident on its armored shield.

Resistance nest WN68 in the D-3 Moulins draw was equipped with two of these VK.3001 tank turrets, designed for an abortive heavy tank that preceded the more famous Tiger. The surplus turrets were dispatched to Normandy for beach defense.

Another view of the VK.3001 turret in WN68. The second turret in this strongpoint had not been fully emplaced on D-Day and was discovered afterwards.

The German 352nd Infantry Division deployed some of its 75mm PaK 40 antitank guns in shorefront gun pits like this example on Omaha.

This aerial view of Dog Green shows the landing area between the St. Laurent and Vierville strongpoints. The tanks on the beach are from the 743rd Tank Battalion, which was much more successful in landing safely compared to its neighbor to the east, the 741st. Its tanks deployed mainly to the east of the Vierville draw because of the heavy antitank-gun fire coming from the bunkers in resistance nest WN72.

LCT(A)-2273 is seen carrying deep-wading M4 tanks of Company A, 743rd Tank Battalion, to the Vierville draw area of Omaha Beach on the morning of D-Day. This craft was damaged by German shore fire, splitting in half and sinking later in the day.

Flotilla 4 heads for Uncle Red Beach in the Utah Beach sector around 0900 hours on D-Day. LCT-495 in the center of this photo was carrying the M7 105mm howitzer motor carriage of Battery B, 65th Field Artillery Battalion.

The deadliest sector of Omaha was Strongpoint Vierville on the western side of the beach, where the 116th Infantry, 29th Division, landed. This section was dominated by a Rgl. Nr. 677 bunker of resistance nest WN72 armed with an 88mm PaK 43/41 that knocked out numerous tanks of the 743rd Tank Battalion during the morning, along with a number of landing craft. This is the view from inside the bunker looking eastward, and as can be seen, the gun could reach virtually all of the beach.

This is a view of the 88mm bunker in WN72, taken after the fighting from its western side. The front of the bunker was disguised to look like the old casino located near this port before the war; the gun faced eastward for enfilade fire along the whole beach.

The eastern side of the WN72 88mm gun bunker as seen a few days after D-Day. Tank and destroyer fire inflicted an enormous amount of damage. This bunker still exists and forms the base of the current U.S. National Guard monument.

A view inside the WN72 88mm bunker, taken several years ago by the author. The 88mm PaK 43/41 gun is still inside the bunker, but it has been pushed deep inside and the embrasure covered over. This image provides a clear idea of the amount of fire directed at the bunkers. Very heavy damage can be seen to the left.

The 88mm bunker in WN72 was supported by another gun bunker slightly to the west that was armed with a 50mm pedestal gun as well as a small Renault FT tank turret. The 50mm gun was positioned to fire out of embrasures pointing either east or west. The small tank turret was on the other side of the bunker and was blown away by tank fire early in the battle.

The two concrete bunkers in WN72 were supported by a 75mm PaK 40 antitank gun deployed in a cave on the cliffs farther inside the Vierville draw, which also had a commanding view of the beach.

The German 352nd Infantry Division attempted to stage an armored counter-attack against the beachhead using its company of Marder III Ausf. M 75mm tank destroyers. They were spotted by navy observation aircraft, and the attack was smashed by naval gunfire.

This LCT was hit by German artillery fire and burned near the beach along with its cargo from an antiaircraft battalion, including an M16 in the foreground, a jeep to the right, and an M15A1 toward the front.

The Dog White section of Omaha Beach is littered with shattered vehicles and craft at low tide on the evening of 6 June 1944. The M4 tank, *C-13 Ceaseless*, is from Company C, 743rd Tank Battalion, and was disabled on the beach after losing a track. The other two companies of tanks from this battalion were M4A1 duplex-drive amphibious tanks.

The beaches between Omaha and Utah around the Vire estuary were especially heavily defended. This is a typical *Panzerstellung* defense work in Grand Vey, fitted with an APX-R turret from a captured French tank.

This is a typical 50mm pedestal gun mount in a *Ringstand*, a type of antitank defense that was ubiquitous along the lower Normandy coast, in this case near Grand Vey.

One of the more widely used turrets for coastal defense in Normandy was the old Renault FT turret like this example on a "Tobruk" *Panzerstellung* in the harbor of Grandcamps-les-Bains immediately to the west of Omaha.

German beach defenses at Utah Beach were much more successfully suppressed by the preliminary air attack and naval gunfire. This is a Rgl. Nr. 667 50mm antitank gun bunker at Utah.

This French 47mm Model 1937 antitank gun was positioned in an open pit in the W5 resistance nest in the dunes near La Madeleine on Utah. Exposed weapons like this were extremely vulnerable to the preparatory bombardment.

Although there were a number of 88mm gun bunkers near Utah Beach, none had the clear field of fire of their two counterparts at Omaha. This is an interior view of one of the 88mm PaK 43/41 bunkers to the northwest of Utah.

The tank landings at Utah went much more smoothly than at Omaha, with the 70th Tank Battalion supporting the 4th Infantry Division's attack. *Cannonball* from Company C, 70th Tank Battalion, stumbled into a shell crater and became trapped. This tank was one of those originally fitted with the T40 Whiz-Bang rocket launcher for use in attacking the German beach obstructions. The mounting for the launcher assembly can be seen on the turret side, and the sight can be seen in front of the commander's hatch.

This disabled Donald Duck tank from Company A, 70th Tank Battalion, was disabled on one of the causeways leading off Utah and was pushed over the side to allow other vehicles to pass.

The Goliath remote-control mines were deployed with several German static-defense divisions on the Normandy coast in the weeks prior to D-Day. They were not widely used in combat, often because of the disruption of the wire-control link. These were found by American troops near Utah.

Another view of a group of Goliath mines near Utah. These were supposed to be used to attack landing craft and tanks along the beach.

The Goliaths were deployed in small hidden caves along the beach. Attempts by the WN5 strongpoint at Utah Beach to use their Goliaths failed when the Allied preparatory bombardment severed the wire-control lines leading to the command bunker.

Paratroopers from the 506th Parachute Infantry Regiment of the 101st Airborne Division cluster around a Renault UE light armored tractor captured near Ravenoville. These small armored vehicles were widely used by the German army in Normandy, and the paratroopers used several over the next few days for miscellaneous chores, mostly hauling supplies.

The 82nd and 101st Airborne Divisions had no armored vehicles and were tightly weight-restricted in their equipment. Antitank defense was provided by special lightweight British 6-pounder Mk. III antitank guns towed by jeeps, as seen here in a village in Normandy after the airborne landings on D-Day.

The Normandy beaches soon grew clogged with traffic as wave after wave of units arrived over the next several days to reinforce the beachhead. Evident in this view of Utah Beach is a 57mm antitank gun in the lower right, an M29 Weasel tracked utility vehicle, and an M4 tank with wading trunks on the horizon.

Another view of Utah Beach as DUKW amphibious trucks bring supplies ashore. Bulldozers on the shore are used to grade paths past the dunes and to assist in the landing.

The scene on Utah later in the day as more and more equipment arrives. The column of M4 tanks with wading trunks is probably from the 746th Tank Battalion, which began landing on Utah shortly before noon on D-Day after the beach had mostly been captured.

A view from the water as the 746th Tank Battalion moves ashore. Unlike the assault waves, all the tank companies in this battalion had deep-wading trunks and no DD tanks.

An M3A1 half-track of the 17th Armored Engineer Battalion, 2nd Armored Division, moves off the beach on D+2.

Infantry comes ashore from an LCVP (landing craft, vehicle, personnel) on Utah Beach. On shore are some M2 half-tracks towing 57mm antitank guns.

Hurricane, an M4 with wading trunks from Company H, 66th Armored Regiment, 2nd Armored Division, comes ashore at Utah Beach on D+2 from an LST. The wading trunks were added to many tanks since the LSTs could often not make it all the way to the beach. The wading trunks allowed the tank to be dropped in water deeper than its hull roofs since the wading trunks and sealant prevented water from flooding the tank.

Another M4 medium tank of the 2nd Armored Division comes ashore from an LST at Utah on 8 June 1944.

Tanks of Company I, 67th Armored Regiment, 2nd Armored Division, move to the docks in Weymouth, England, prior to transit to Normandy on 10 June 1944. They are already fitted with deep-wading trunks. There is a column of German POWs in the lower right corner, captured in Normandy in the previous three days of fighting. Since the beachhead was not very large, German prisoners for the first few days of the fighting were sent back to England on landing craft returning to pick up other units.

An M3A1 half-track of a towed tank destroyer battalion brings ashore its 3-inch antitank gun at Utah Beach a few days after D-Day. The tank destroyer battalions in Normandy were a mixture of self-propelled battalions with M10 or M18 gun motor carriages and the towed battalions with the 3-inch antitank gun.

An M32B1 named *Shoot Six Bits*, one of the first M32 tank-recovery vehicles on French soil, exits from the Utah Beach area in Normandy in June 1944.

An M7 105mm howitzer motor carriage with full deep-wading fittings comes ashore in Normandy, with an LCT visible in the background.

An M2 half-track car towing a trailer comes ashore from an LCT on Utah Beach on 15 June.

M4 tanks with wading trunks of the 3rd Armored Division are prepared in England before departing for Normandy. The division arrived in France in the last week of June 1944.

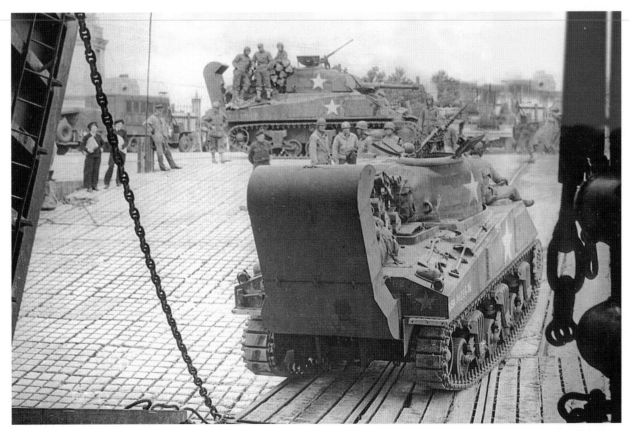

A pair of M4 tanks of the 3rd Armored Division load aboard an LST for transit to Normandy in late June 1944. They are fitted with the standard deep-wading trunks.

CHAPTER 3

The Battle for Normandy

THE U.S. ARMY WAS UNPREPARED for the battlefield conditions that followed the Normandy landings, having underestimated the effects of the dense hedgerows, called *bocage*. The *bocage* formed a natural defensive barrier to a war of maneuver, and American operations were severely constrained by the terrain. As a result, most of the combat in the first month of the Normandy campaign was dominated by close-range infantry fighting. There were numerous small-scale tank actions in support of infantry, but few above company size. The terrain problems were not restricted to the U.S. Army. When the Wehrmacht attempted to launch panzer counterattacks against the American beachhead, such as that by the Panzer Lehr Division on 11 July, these too proved to be severely limited by the defensive advantages of the *bocage*, and the Panzer Lehr took heavy losses.

At a considerable cost in men and materiel, the U.S. Army gradually began to adapt to the new terrain, capturing the port of Cherbourg by the end of June and the vital road junction of St. Lô by mid-July. The Wehrmacht concentrated most of its panzer divisions farther east in the better tank country around Caen, fearing the threat of a British armored breakout. By mid-July, the American sector was defended by one full-strength panzer division (the 2nd SS Panzer Division) and two other divisions that had become badly beat up in the *bocage* fighting (the Panzer Lehr Division and the 17th SS Panzer Grenadier Division). By this stage, the U.S. Army had two armored divisions in Normandy with Bradley's First Army (the 2nd and 3rd Armored Divisions), and two more were added when Patton's Third Army was secretly transferred from the United Kingdom (the 4th and 6th Armored Divisions). These provided the vital mass of maneuver needed for a new operation, code-named Cobra, which was intended to rip open the thinly defended German lines and secure a breakout from Normandy.

In anticipation of the breakout operation, the U.S. Army deployed one of its secret weapons. American units had been experimenting with various types of devices to permit a tank to crash through the dense *bocage*. Called "rhinos" or Culin hedgerow cutters, these came in a broader range of shapes and types than is generally realized. More than 600 of these were locally manufactured in mid-July and fastened to the front of many tanks.

A glider infantryman from the 82nd Airborne Division stands guard near the wreck of a German Renault UE light armored tractor on 14 June 1944. This is near the glider landing zones. A Waco CG-4A glider can be seen behind the foliage.

A paratrooper inspects a German fortified position about a mile behind Utah Beach in the airborne landing zones. The tank wreck in the foreground is a French Renault R-35 light tank. It was overturned by naval gunfire and was probably from Panzer Abteilung 100 (100th Tank Battalion), which was active in fighting with the 82nd Airborne Division behind the beachhead in the days after the landings.

American units continued to face German coastal defenses as they fought their way up along the Cotentin Peninsula toward Cherbourg in June 1944. This is a 50mm pedestal gun in a *Ringstand* fortification knocked out during the fighting around Fort de Foucarville up the coast from Utah.

A wrecked German Marder III tank destroyer in a town square during the early fighting in the Utah Beach sector. This type of vehicle was widely used in the Normandy campaign, with each German infantry division nominally having a company of these.

A German Marder III tank destroyer moves up on the Normandy front past the damaged wing of a Horsa glider. This German photo was found by an officer of the U.S. 1st Infantry Division.

On D+1, Grenadier Regiment 1058, supported by several StuG III Ausf. G assault guns, attempted to overcome the 82nd Airborne Division's defenses in Sainte-Mère-Église. They were counter-attacked by elements of the HQ Company and Company B, 746th Tank Battalion. As can be seen, the attack was beaten back with the loss of two assault guns and some towed antitank guns.

A view of the German armored column from the other direction toward Sainte-Mère-Église shows the ill-fated German column.

The other StuG III Ausf. G knocked out while supporting Grenadier Regiment 1058's attacks on U.S. paratroopers in Sainte-Mère-Église. This one was hit no fewer than four times, but from the size of the gouges on the bow, it was probably a victim of M4 tanks of the 746th Tank Battalion. An airborne 57mm antitank gun sits beside it.

During their attack, the column from the 746th Tank Battalion lost two M4 tanks to German antitank fire. Here they are passed by paratroop infantry.

A paratrooper from the 82nd Airborne Division examines one of the M4 medium tanks from the 746th Tank Battalion knocked out in the Sainte-Mère-Église fighting.

GIs of the 4th Infantry Division escort a group of German prisoners as an M4 medium tank of the 70th Tank Battalion passes by during the fighting west of Sainte-Mère-Église on 10 June as part of the VII Corps' effort to expand the Utah beachhead toward Cherbourg.

The airborne division had relatively weak antitank capabilities, relying on bazookas and small numbers of 6-pounder (57mm) antitank guns. Nevertheless, these proved adequate to beat off an armored attack by the 17th SS Panzer Grenadier Division near Carentan, as seen here with a knocked-out StuG IV assault gun behind a 6-pounder of the 82nd Airborne Division on 13 June.

An M4 tank of Company A, 746th Tank Battalion, passes through St. Sauveur-le-Vicomte during the fighting in Normandy in June. This unit was used to support the 82nd Airborne Division during the initial fighting that month.

A column of M5A1 light tanks—probably from Company D, 746th Tank Battalion—advances through a Norman village in June 1944. At this stage of the war, each U.S. Army tank battalion had a single company of these light tanks.

This Marder III Ausf. M from Panzerjäger Abteilung 243 (243rd Tank Destroyer Battalion) was captured by the 82nd Airborne Division during the fighting on the Cotentin Peninsula in Normandy in June 1944. A knocked-out M4 medium tank can be seen in front of it.

American troops occasionally found personal photos taken by German soldiers, like this shot of a converted French Lorraine tractor with a 150mm howitzer of the 21st Panzer Division in France. These vehicles operated mainly in the neighboring British sector of the Normandy front.

An M7 105mm howitzer motor carriage moves to the front in Normandy on 13 June as part of the efforts to expand the beachhead.

Armored D9 dozers were used by U.S. Army engineer units in Normandy, seen here clearing debris in a Norman town.

The Möbelwagen mated the 37mm FlaK 36 with the Pz.Kpfw. IV chassis and was first encountered by the U.S. Army in Normandy in June 1944. This example has the side panels folded down.

An M7 105mm howitzer motor carriage of Battery B, 14th Armored Field Artillery Battalion, 2nd Armored Division, moves through Carentan on 18 June. This vehicle is the intermediate-production type with the deeper pulpit introduced in January 1943. The 2nd Armored Division added stowage racks on the hull side, much like those on half-tracks.

Troops of the 3rd Armored Division take a breather in front of one of the division's M4 tanks near Le Desert, France, on 31 July 1944.

A U.S. Army mechanized column passes through Montebourg on 23 June as the local citizens wave. The M3A1 half-track to the left is nicknamed *Dirty Gertie*.

GIs inspect a 4.7-centimeter PaK(t) auf Pz.Kpfw. 35R(f), a tank destroyer consisting of a Czechoslovakian 47mm gun mounted on a French Renault R-35 chassis. There were 110 of these in service in France in 1944, mainly in Normandy. This one was abandoned in Littry and was photographed on 20 June 1944.

Another example of a 47mm PaK(t) auf Pz.Kpfw. 35R(f) captured in Normandy. These were used by a number of German tank destroyer companies in lower Normandy in the summer of 1944.

A rear view of the same vehicle from a wartime technical intelligence report on captured German equipment. The Normandy garrison received a number of these conversions on old French tank chassis in 1943 when this front had low priority for equipment; by 1944, they were becoming obsolete.

A U.S. ordnance collection point for captured German equipment in lower Normandy shows the usual mixture of types typical in this theater in June. In the background is an old French Hotchkiss H-39 tank that was probably used by Panzer Abteilung 100 during the fighting with the paratroopers. The tank destroyer in the upper right is a Panzerjäger 38(t) Ausf. H, which was armed with the effective 75mm PaK 40 antitank gun. In the foreground is a pair of Renault UE light armored tractors that were widely used by the German army in Normandy for utility tasks.

An M32B1 tank-recovery vehicle (named *Step N' Fetchit* after the popular radio character) passes through the town of Sainte-Mère-Église on 21 June during the fighting for St. Lô. It is towing an M4 medium tank. There were five M31 or M32 tank-recovery vehicles in each tank battalion—one in each of the three medium tank companies and two with the battalion's service company.

An M4 composite-hull medium tank extracts itself from a muddy irrigation ditch alongside a hedgerow in late June. The *bocage* so characteristic of this section of Normandy made tank operations especially difficult in the first month of fighting.

The commander of a well-camouflaged M4 medium tank peers through binoculars during the fighting on the Cotentin Peninsula in mid-June 1944 during the advance toward Cherbourg.

The troops in an armored recon jeep talks to local French civilians while patrolling on the outskirts of Cherbourg on 17 July.

The port city of Cherbourg on the northern tip of the Cotentin Peninsula was a major objective of the VII Corps in the last weeks of June. This port was heavily defended by German fortifications, and this is one of the typical German 50mm pedestal guns in a *Ringstand* concrete pit, typical of German coastal defenses in Normandy.

A GI bazooka team poses next to the armored cupola of a German bunker in the outer-defense belt that ringed the port of Cherbourg.

An M4 tank from the 740th Tank Battalion supports a group of GIs during the street fighting in Cherbourg, which began in earnest on 21 June with an assault by the U.S. 4th and 79th Divisions.

An M4 of the 746th Tank Battalion moves down Rue du Val de Saire in Cherbourg on 26 June during the fighting there.

A pair of M4 tanks of the 740th Tank Battalion moves through Cherbourg on 27 June. This was the first Normandy port to fall into Allied hands, but the Germans had so thoroughly demolished its facilities that it was of little benefit to the Allies for months.

An M4 medium tank (named *Big-Bad-Momma*) of Company B, 740th Tank Battalion, is serviced by its crew in Cherbourg after the port city fell earlier in the month. For the first three months of the French campaign, the M4 and M4A1 medium tanks were the predominant types in U.S. Army service. The newer, and preferred, M4A3 did not begin to appear in large numbers until the late summer.

A U.S. Army military police patrol use a captured Kettenkrad tracked motorcycle while on duty in the seaport of Cherbourg after its capture in late June 1944.

A GI inspects a column of German Renault UE light armored tractors abandoned in Cherbourg following the surrender of the port. These French vehicles had originally been built by the French army in the 1930s to tow 25mm antitank guns.

GIs and local French civilians enjoy the liberation of Cherbourg while driving around on a Renault UE light armored tractor on 29 June.

Captured UE light armored tractors were sometimes used by American troops after their capture. This example was modified by the 9th Air Service Command ordnance for airfield protection in Normandy by adding a gun shield along with a German aircraft machine gun found on a captured airfield.

An M4 tank supporting troops near Haye-du-Poits on 7 July. This is a relatively early-production M4 with the initial gun-mantlet configuration without the side-cheek armor. It has been rebuilt with the added hull and turret armor, probably in England. The use of the prominent Allied star was common in the initial phases of the Normandy fighting, but they were later painted out by most units since they provided too inviting a target to German gunners.

A well-camouflaged M4 of the 70th Tank Battalion is passed by a medic's jeep during the fighting in the Normandy hedgerows in July 1944. During the campaign, the 70th Tank Battalion provided support to the 4th Infantry Division.

An M1A1 heavy wrecker truck of the 9th Air Service Command is used to extract a damaged German StuG III assault gun from a ditch in Normandy in early July.

A StuG III Ausf G. found destroyed along the roadside in France in July 1944. This was one of the most commonly encountered German armored vehicles in the American sector of the Normandy front.

Troops of the 117th Infantry, 30th Division, supported by an M4A1 Donald Duck tank of the 743rd Tank Battalion, move through St. Fromond on 7 July during the offensive toward the Vire River. This tank is a veteran of the D-Day landings in the Vierville sector, but it has had its canvas screen removed.

An M5A1 (named *L-on-Wheels*) from Company L, 32nd Armored Regiment, Combat Command A (CCA), 3rd Armored Division, passes by a 90mm antiaircraft gun set up for improvised antitank defense in St. Fromond on July 9. The tank is heading toward Le Desert, where the Panzer Lehr Division was conducting a major counterattack. Curiously enough, it is still fitted with the canvas waterproofing over the 37mm gun.

The crew of an M5A1 (named *Cadallac*) of Company C, 33rd Armored Regiment, 3rd Armored Division, looks at the effects of a near artillery miss on the sheet-metal sand shields.

An M10 of the 823rd Tank Destroyer Battalion in support of the 30th Division during the advance through St. Fromond on 7 July.

A column from CCB of the U.S. 3rd Armored Division ran into elements of the 6th Company of SS Panzer Regiment 2 of the 2nd SS Panzer Division supporting Kampfgruppe Wisliceny near St. Fromond, where the Germans lost several Pz.Kpfw. IV tanks.

CCB, 3rd Armored Division, passes the knocked-out German column. The tank in the foreground is an M4A1 medium tank (named *Derby*) of Company D, 33rd Armored Regiment.

A view down the road as an M4A1 medium tank of the 33rd Armored Regiment passes by two knocked-out Pz.Kpfw. IV tanks of the 6th Company, SS Panzer Regiment 2. The rear tank is numbered 622 and carries the divisional insignia in the upper-left corner of the rear plate.

An M5A1 light tank of Company C, 3rd Battalion, 33rd Armored Regiment, CCB, 3rd Armored Division, passes along the same stretch of road in St. Fromond on 11 July while the fighting in this sector continued.

An M10 3-inch gun motor carriage from the 703rd Tank Destroyer Battalion supports the 3rd Armored Division near St. Jean de Daye on 11 July. That day, the Panzer Lehr Division launched a counterattack in this sector, and the tank destroyers were credited with knocking out ten Panthers and a Pz.Kpfw. IV. This vehicle has the tactical number A21 painted on the side, along with the vehicle name *Accident*, identifying it as a tank destroyer of Company A.

The Panzer Lehr Division staged a number of attacks in the difficult *bocage* country through July, losing large numbers of tanks. From a starting strength of ninety-nine Pz.Kpfw. IV and eighty-nine Panthers, it had been reduced to only fifteen operational Pz.Kpfw. IV and sixteen Panthers at the time Operation Cobra began. This Panther was knocked out by a 57mm antitank gun and was photographed near St. Lô on 20 July. No fewer than four penetrations can be seen near the driver's station.

Another view of the Panther Ausf. A of the Panzer Lehr Division that was knocked out by a 57mm antitank gun. Although the Panther was invulnerable to the 57mm gun frontally, it was very vulnerable on the side.

A pair of Panthers block a narrow country lane in Le Desert after the failed Panzer Lehr Division's counterattack of 11 July.

The constricted hedgerow terrain of Normandy presented significant difficulties in deploying antitank guns since the hedges often rose over the height of the gun barrel and restricted traverse. This 57mm gun is seen deployed behind a hedgerow in July 1944. Although incapable of penetrating the frontal armor of a Panther, these guns did prove effective on numerous occasions when firing from the flank.

The bazooka proved to be an effective, though not entirely reliable, antitank weapon in the *bocage* fighting. It was best when used at relatively close ranges and when fired at the thinner side armor of German tanks.

A very clear example of why a Sherman was not a good match for a Panther. This particular M4A1 engaged in an unequal duel with a Panther from the Panzer Lehr Division and is seen here on 20 July after the German panzer offensive had been beaten back. Besides the six hits from the Panther's 75mm gun, there are two smaller holes on the M4A1 from Panzerfaust or Panzerschreck rocket launchers.

The Panzer Lehr's attack in July marked a shift of German resources, which had been concentrated largely around Caen to stop the British and Canadian attacks. This Panther was knocked out in the Caen sector in early July by a PIAT (projector, infantry, antitank), the standard British infantry antitank weapon.

British and Canadian tank losses around Caen were heavy. These Shermans were knocked out during fighting with the 1st SS Panzer Division around Caen; the tank in the background is a 17-pounder Firefly version with the improved armament.

A battery of the new M4 (105mm) assault guns provide fire support during the fighting in the approaches to St. Lô on 13 July. The M4 (105mm) assault gun was a version of the normal Sherman, but was fitted with a 105mm howitzer in the turret instead of the usual 75mm gun. These were used in tank battalion and tank company headquarters platoons for additional fire support. They were first deployed in Normandy on 3 July, and on 13 July, there were forty-seven in action with the U.S. First Army in Normandy—an average of six each in eight separate tank battalions.

On 14 July, an M31 tank-recovery vehicle recovers an M4 of the 3rd Armored Division that was knocked out in the fighting on 11 July around St. Fromond. The large turret tactical numbers are typical of both the 2nd and 3rd Armored Divisions during the *bocage* fighting.

A Patterson conversion on an M2 half-track of the 377th Anti-Aircraft Artillery Automatic-Weapons Battalion is being used to provide fire support for an infantry unit in Normandy on 12 July. As can be seen from the open side door, the usual stowage bin inside the M2 has been removed to permit this conversion. The Patterson conversions were an effort to create expedient M16 machine-gun motor carriage done in England before D-Day by mounting towed quad .50-caliber Maxson turrets on the chassis of surplus M2 half-tracks. They were a rough equivalent of the factory-built M16 antiaircraft half-track but can be distinguished by the lack of a folding side plate and the shorter hull.

A wrecker truck is used to remove a 3-inch gun from an M10 3-inch gun motor carriage tank destroyer in a repair area in Normandy in mid-July. The M4 medium tank in the background is probably from the 2nd Armored Division.

A German Sd.Kfz. 222 armored car knocked out by the 1st Battalion, 8th Infantry, during the fighting on the approaches to St. Lô on 15 July. The armor on the rear of the vehicle has been blown off, exposing the engine.

A Marder III Ausf. M tank destroyer hit by American artillery fire is inspected by a GI from the unit on 18 July.

An ordnance repair yard handles battle casualties on 18 July. The M4A1 tank numbered 16 is named *Anne* and is from Company A, 70th Tank Battalion. The M4 numbered I-35 is named *Intruder* and is from one of the armored regiments of the 3rd Armored Division. To the far left is an M10 3-inch gun motor carriage tank destroyer.

A Patterson conversion based on an M2 half-track of the 456th Anti-Aircraft Artillery Automatic-Weapons Battalion (Mobile) is seen knocked out in *bocage* country on the outskirts of St. Lô during the fighting there in mid-July. The crew has added a stowage rack on the rear shelf, a typical improvisation on the M2 half-track.

An M12 155mm gun motor carriage (named *June Gil*) of the 991st Armored Field Artillery Battalion in action on 16 July during the St. Lô fighting. The French inscription on the hull side: *Avant le char de mort!* means "Forward tank of death!"

Corregidor, an M12 155mm gun motor carriage from the 991st Field Artillery Battalion, fires on targets near St. Lô on 16 July, two days after the battalion entered combat. The 991st was a descendant of the famous "Washington Greys" regiment and continued the unit traditions with its regimental shield painted on the superstructure sides.

A pair of French children wave to the crew of a passing M4 tank of the 3rd Armored Division moving through the town of St. Paul de Verney, east of St. Lô, on 17 July.

An M5A1 (named *Concrete C*12*) of Company C, 33rd Armored Regiment, 3rd Armored Division, passes through St. Paul de Verney on 17 July during the fighting along the Vire River. The 33rd Armored Regiment quickly painted over the stars that had been painted between the yellow company speed number on the hull side; they were too visible an aiming point for German gunners.

The crew of an M4 medium tank set up camp for the night near St. Paul de Verney on 17 July. The tank name *Inez* and letter I on the turret indicate a tank from Company I, 33rd Armored Regiment, 3rd Armored Division. Notice that the American white stars have already been painted out.

The capture of the key road junction at St. Lô was vital to the American plans for Operation Cobra. The city finally fell on 18–19 July, setting the stage for the offensive. In the ruins of the city is a German Sd.Kfz. 231 armored car. This was a relatively old type of reconnaissance vehicle that had been largely replaced with the more modern Sd.Kfz. 234 series by the time of the Normandy campaign.

The M8 light armored cars of the reconnaissance company of the 29th Division in the ruins of St. Lô after its capture.

An M5A1, possibly from the 747th Tank Battalion, in the ruined streets of St. Lô on 20 July. It is already fitted with sandbag armor. Notice also that it still carries sand skirts, a feature that was generally removed in the late summer in the U.S. First Army as a maintenance hindrance.

The problems posed by the *bocage* led to a number of attempts to find a way to crash through the hedgerows. The "salad fork" developed by the 747th Tank Battalion was one of the first attempts to develop such a device. The two pointed timbers created tunnels in the base of the hedge that could be filled with explosives. When detonated by accompanying engineers, a breach was created.

A close up of a "salad fork" on a 747th Tank Battalion Sherman. Although successfully used in combat on a small scale, the tactic required the use of too much high explosive to be practical.

The "Green dozer," also developed by the 747th Tank Battalion, was an attempt to breach the *bocage* by non-explosive means. It consisted of a steel girder made from railroad beams welded on a frame to the front of the tank as a means to plow through the hedges. It was used in small numbers during Operation Cobra by the 709th and 747th Tank Battalions, but was not especially successful.

Sgt. Curtis Culin of the 102nd Cavalry Squadron designed a *bocage* cutter using scrap steel from German beach defenses. This photo shows his original design mounted on an M5A1 from his unit. This was the basis for the "rhino" cutter that was mass-produced by army ordnance units in France for Operation Cobra in July.

Culin's hedge cutter is shown here mounted on an M5A1 light tank.

Culin's "rhino" device was displayed to a number of senior officers on 14 July, as seen here. This demonstration led Gen. Omar Bradley to order the device into large-scale production.

Sgt. Curtis Culin in the driver seat of an M5A1 during the July demonstration.

Most of the "rhino" devices were fitted to M4 medium tanks since they had the weight and power to crunch through the hedgerow. Here is a demonstration in July prior to their operational debut in Cobra.

In this view, the M4 with the "rhino" device has pushed through the test *bocage*.

There were several variations of the T1 Rhinoceros, such as this T1E1 Rhinoceros on an M10 3-inch gun motor carriage. This had an additional prong in the center. The 2nd Armored Division had about three-fifths of their tanks fitted with these devices by the time the offensive started on 25 July.

Another variation on the "rhino" was the T1E2 seen on this M4. This had a more substantial bumper, and the shape of the prongs is a bit different from the more common T1 style.

The 3rd Armored Division used its own distinctive style of "rhino," the T2 Douglas device. It can be distinguished by the triangular plates on either side. This particular example is seen fitted to a late-production M4A1 formerly configured as a DD tank, as is evident from the turret fittings.

This front view of the M4A1 shows the configuration of the T2 Douglas with the smaller "teeth" in the center.

The least common of the "rhino" devices was the T3, seen here fitted to an M4A1. This was the flimsiest of the designs, and it was also fitted to M10 tank destroyers.

There were a number of variations of the "Green dozer," such as the T4 Rhinoceros seen here. This type was not widely seen in use. It was effective in pushing aside brush, but not in plowing through the dense base of the hedgerow.

A T2 Douglas device being fitted to an M4A1 (76mm) of the 32nd Armored, 3rd Armored Division. The new version of the Sherman with the 76mm gun saw its combat debut in Operation Cobra, with the 2nd and 3rd Armored Division each receiving fifty-one of these.

U.S. Army camouflage discipline was notoriously poor, and when some captured German tankers mocked the sloppy American practices, orders were dispatched to remedy the situation before Cobra. So the U.S. First Army's 602nd Engineer Camouflage Battalion began developing a method for permanently attaching Sommerfield matting to tanks so that foliage could be easily attached. This is the pilot, an M4 tank (named *Columbia Lou*) of Company C, 70th Tank Battalion.

This is a demonstration of how the Sommerfield matting was intended to be used once foliage was attached. In practice, there was not enough time to carry this program out very extensively, so instead, the U.S. First Army adopted a program to paint as many of its tanks as possible in a pattern of black over the usual olive drab in the days before the start of Cobra.

CHAPTER 4

Operation Cobra: The Normandy Breakout

OPERATION COBRA BEGAN with a carpet-bombing attack against the thinly stretched Panzer Lehr Division that obliterated the division's forward defenses, as will become very evident from the following photos. Its Panther tank battalion was deployed forward along the main line of resistance and was largely annihilated. Its Panzer IV battalion was farther to the rear, but suffered heavy losses in the fighting that ensued. The U.S. Army's separate tank battalions had worked out new tactics using their secret Culin hedgerow cutters and were able to plow through the *bocage* and slowly but relentlessly push past the German defenses. Once the initial German main line had been penetrated by a combined tank-infantry assault, the 2nd and 3rd Armored Divisions were launched deep behind the German lines.

After weeks of stalemate, the German army underestimated the mobile potential of the American armored units. In hopes of preserving the remaining panzers for a counterattack, the German Seventh Army's commander directed their withdrawal toward the road junction at Percy, unwittingly positioning them to be surrounded. During the last week of July, the 2nd SS Panzer Division and the remnants of the 17th SS Panzer Grenadier Division were cut off, and much of their armored equipment was lost in the encirclement battle with the U.S. 2nd Armored Division around Roncey. Although the Roncey pocket is not as well known as the later Falaise pocket, the Germans' losses here crippled their defenses in the American sector.

While the U.S. First Army was dealing with the remnants of the German Seventh Army, Patton's new Third Army was injected into the crumbling defenses near the coast, racing westward for Avranches, the gateway into Brittany. Allied planning had made the capture of the Breton ports one of its key summer objectives. The 4th Armored Division raced across the base of the peninsula, cutting it off from further reinforcement, while the 6th Armored Division made one of the fastest and deepest advances in U.S. Army history, isolating the key port at Brest.

A column of tanks from the 2nd Armored Division uses the cover of a tree line near Champ du Bouet while awaiting orders prior to the start of Operation Cobra. The lead tank is one of the new M4A1 (76mm)'s and—judging from the vehicle number, E-1—is probably a Company E commander's tank.

In preparation for the start of Cobra, M29 Weasels were used as resupply vehicles loading 4.2-inch smoke ammunition for Company C, 87th Chemical Battalion, U.S. First Army, in the Normandy *bocage* on 24 July.

The tiny M29 Weasel was sometimes used as an improvised troop carrier as seen here on 24 July, with vehicles supporting Company C, 87th Chemical Battalion.

An M2 half-track follows behind an M5A1 light tank through a village near St. Lô on 25 July while moving forward to the start line.

Operation Cobra began at 1300 hours on 24 July with a massive carpet-bombing attack along the D900 St.Lô–Périers highway by 1,495 B-17 and B-24 bombers. This is a rare view of the strike, looking toward the west with the bomb impacts in the lower left covering the area around Chapelle-en-Juger near the intersection of Routes D900 and D972. A pair of B-24 bombers is in the upper right.

The carpet-bombing that opened Cobra targeted the Panzer Lehr Division, which had fewer than a dozen Panther tanks strung out in a thin defensive belt south of St. Lô. The attack caused heavy casualties among the leading edge of the division, as is evident from this overturned Panther.

A Panther tank knocked out during the St. Lô breakout. There is a distinct shell gouge on its glacis plate, so this may have been knocked out in fighting rather than by the bombing attack.

U.S. Army engineers sweep for mines around one of the Panther tanks knocked out along the St. Lô–Périers road by the Cobra bombing.

A view of the same Panther from the other side reveals that the bomb attack penetrated the upper-right corner of the hull armor.

GIs clamber over the Panther for a closer look. It is not clear if this Panther was knocked into the ditch by bombing or shoved off a road by tractors.

A Panther with its turret knocked off along the St. Lô–Périers road.

This close-up of the Panther with the dislodged turret suggests an internal ammunition fire that detonated inside the vehicle as the plate over the driver's compartment is also blown off. There was an ammunition bin under the center of this panel.

A view of the Panther from the front as GIs inspect the wreckage.

GIs pose next to a knocked-out Panther of the Panzer Lehr Division along the St. Lô–Périers road. One of the GIs has extracted some clothing from inside the tank.

A close-up of the demolished Panther while the GIs pose for the camera.

A day after the initial bombing, GIs inspect some of the equipment abandoned by the Panzer Lehr Division along the St. Lô–Périers road after the carpet-bombing. In the foreground is an Sd.Kfz. 251/7 armored half-track fitted with engineer bridging equipment, and behind it is a disabled Panther Ausf. A. A few Panthers survived the initial bombing but were quickly overwhelmed by the ensuing infantry attack.

A GI poses in front of another of the Panzer Lehr's Panthers knocked out at the start of Cobra.

GIs advance past a destroyed Panther, perhaps the same one as in a previous photo. The irregular surface on the Panther is Zimmerit, a type of cement coating applied to many German tanks from 1943 as an antidote to Russian magnetic antitank mines.

OPERATION COBRA: THE NORMANDY BREAKOUT **125**

The Panzer Lehr had only about sixteen Panther tanks operational when Cobra started, and by the end of the campaign, it had none. This one is another victim of the preliminary air bombardment.

Another view along the St. Lô–Périers road, where the Cobra carpet-bombing has overturned an Sd.Kfz. 251 half-track.

Later on 25 July 1944, the 2nd Armored Division overran other depleted elements of the Panzer Lehr Division, including this Pz.Kpfw. IV with tactical number 841.

A view of the same Panzer Lehr Pz.Kpfw. IV from the opposite side as a column from the 2nd Armored Division passes by. Of the seventy Pz.Kpfw. IV in service at the beginning of July, the Panzer Lehr had only fifteen left by 1 August.

One of the new M4A1 (76mm)'s is seen breaking over the top of a hedgerow near Pont Hebert during the opening phases of Cobra. A total of 102 of these were split evenly between the 2nd and 3rd Armored Divisions when first delivered on 22 July. It was hoped that the 76mm gun would be the trick in dealing with the Panther, but Cobra showed that it was inadequate when dealing with the well-angled frontal armor of the Panther.

An M4A1 (76mm) of the 3rd Armored Division fitted with a T2 Douglas device in operations near Reffeuville on 25 July at the start of Operation Cobra.

An M4 tank moves down a road in Normandy on 25 July. To the left is an overturned Sd.Kfz. 251, probably one of the vehicles from the Panzer Lehr Division that was hit in the carpet-bombing attack.

One of the key pieces of equipment during Cobra was the M1 bulldozer blade, seen here fitted to *Apache* from Company A, 70th Tank Battalion, near Tribehou on 25 July. Although the Culin prongs are more famous, the bulldozer blades were in fact more effective. Each of the separate tank battalions was provided with five or six tank dozers for the Cobra breakout.

A close-up of a 70th Tank Battalion dozer tank named *Here's Dots Mom* is seen pushing through hedgerow.

A day after the start of Cobra, an M8 75mm howitzer motor carriage of the 3rd Armored Division passes by the wreckage of an overturned M4 tank near Marigny on 26 July. The M4 has suffered an internal ammunition fire which has blown out floor panels.

German units in Normandy made extensive use of the Sturmgeschütz, a turretless assault gun based on panzer chassis. There were about 190 StuG's operational in Normandy at the start of Cobra, of which about a third were in the Seventh Army's sector facing the U.S. First Army. This is a StuG IV based on the Pz.Kpfw. IV chassis, which was less common than the StuG III in Normandy. This particular vehicle served with SS Panzer Abteilung 17 of the 17th SS Panzer Grenadier Division and was hit by Ninth Air Force fighter-bombers along the Marigny-Montrevil road.

Another view of the destruction along the Marigny-Montrevil road caused by Ninth Air Force fighter-bombers. On the right is a burnt-out Panther, while a Pz.Kpfw. IV lies in the mud off the road.

An Sd.Kfz. 250/8 Schützenpanzerwagen (2cm) knocked out along the Marigny-Montrevil road. This was the reconnaissance version of the Sd.Kfz. 250 half-track family and intended to replace the earlier Sd.Kfz. 222 wheeled armored car.

The onrush of the 2nd and 3rd Armored Divisions on 26 July overwhelmed a number of German armored units in their path. This smoldering StuG IV, probably from the 17th SS Panzer Grenadier Division, is passed by an American M2A1 half-track.

An M4A1 (76mm) (named *Duke*) of Company D, 66th Armored Regiment, 2nd Armored Division, carries an infantry team into action during Operation Cobra. During the first few days of the campaign, it was the practice in the 2nd Armored Division to carry a team of armored infantry on the tanks to assist in the breakthrough. This tank has the new First Army black and olive-drab camouflage pattern adopted in anticipation of Cobra.

This StuG IV became trapped in a ditch along a hedgerow on the Marigny-Montrevil road and was abandoned during fighting on 27 July.

An M5A1 light tank moves forward during Cobra. It is finished in the standard First Army camouflage scheme. The tanker manning the .30-caliber light machine gun has stuck an M1 steel helmet over the usual tanker's helmet for head protection. The tanker's normal helmet offered no ballistic protection, and there were many field expedients by American tankers to remedy this problem.

A pair of M5A1's of Company B, 33rd Armored Regiment, 3rd Armored Division, races down a road near Marigny on 26 July. This was part of the Combat Command B spearhead that collided later in the day with a force from the 2nd SS Panzer Division.

An M4 passes by a Panther knocked out near La Chapelle during Cobra.

An M8 75mm howitzer motor carriage leads a column from the reconnaissance company of the 33rd Armored Regiment, 3rd Armored Division, at Montreuil-sur-Lozon on 26 July. CCB of the 3rd Armored Division was committed that day to support the attack of the 1st Infantry Division.

A platoon of M4A1 (76mm) tanks, probably from the 2nd Armored Division, undergoes repairs in the town square of St. Jean de Daye on 26 July. The new 76mm gun was not well received when first issued to American tank units as its high-explosive projectile was not as effective as the type available with the 75mm gun. The 76mm gun was better appreciated in July when tank units began encountering the thickly armored Panther in greater numbers.

CCA of the 2nd Armored Division reached the road junction at Canisy by the late afternoon of 26 July, after part of the town had been set ablaze by an air attack. There was little resistance from the shattered Panzer Lehr Division. This is an M8 armored car of the division's 82nd Reconnaissance Battalion.

The crew of an M8 light armored car (named *Danny*) scan for German forces after reaching the road junction in Canisy. They are from the 82nd Reconnaissance Battalion that was spearheading the drive southward past the shattered remains of the Panzer Lehr.

An M4 tank, probably from the 712th Tank Battalion, which was supporting the 90th Division during the attack, moves through the contested town of Périers on 27 July, with an M10 3-inch gun motor carriage tank destroyer behind it.

Traffic jams in the French towns south and east of St. Lô were a major hindrance once the breakout began, and MP jeeps were out in force to enforce traffic order, as seen here on 29 July. In the background is one of the new M4 (105mm) assault guns, probably from 37th Tank Battalion, 4th Armored Division, judging from the markings.

This StuG IV, probably from the 17th SS Panzer Grenadier Division, was knocked out during fighting near Périers.

A GI walks past an Sd.Kfz. 251 Ausf. D of a towed antitank gun company of the 2nd Panzer Division.

U.S. Army military police direct traffic at an intersection in St. Gilles near the wreckage of two Pz.Kpfw. IV tanks knocked out in the fighting there. The Panzer Lehr had attempted to defend the junction with four Pz.Kpfw. IV tanks and a StuG III, but they were quickly overwhelmed by the 2nd Armored Division.

A Pz.Kpfw. IV knocked out in the Canadian sector between Caen and Vaucelles during the fighting there that culminated in the Falaise pocket in August.

Some idea of the intensity of the aerial bombardment during Cobra can be gathered from this aerial photo, taken days later after the road had been cleared for use by U.S. troops. During the retreat of the 2nd SS Panzer Division, a German column was caught in the open during daylight and hit by medium bombers.

An M4 tank of the 6th Armored Division speeds through Brehal on 27 July, the day armored units of Patton's Third Army were injected into the west flank of the advance to race for the access roads to Brittany.

An M4 fitted with the Culin prongs passes by an M10 3-inch gun motor carriage during the opening phases of Cobra in late July 1944.

An M5A1 (named *Wasp*) of a battalion HQ from 32nd Armored, 3rd Armored Division, passes through a shattered town on 27 July. It has the characteristic 3rd Armored Division's brushguard below the bow machine gun. A typical tactical number 3-11 appears on the hull rear, but it seems to have been painted over. An air ID panel is draped over the rear turret stowage.

Lead elements of CCB of the 2nd Armored Division seized the bridges over the Soulle River at Pont Brocard on 27 July, nearly capturing the commander of the Panzer Lehr in the process. Here, a 57mm antitank gun is stationed at a road junction in the town on 29 July as an M4 medium tank passes by. The 2nd was one of the few American units to wear camouflage battle dress during Cobra, a practice that ended in August because of frequent confusion with German camouflage clothing.

On 28 July, the commander of the German Seventh Army ordered a retreat toward Percy to avoid encirclement. The direction of the withdrawal was ill-advised, and the 2nd SS Panzer Division became encircled around Roncey. In a series of engagements with 2nd Armored Division and U.S. P-47 fighter-bombers, the division lost most of its heavy equipment. Some idea of the carnage on the road back from the roadblock can be seen in this photo taken outside St. Denis-le-Cast the next day. The abandoned hulks of a number of Sd.Kfz. 251 halftracks have already been pushed off the road. The second half-track in the column is an Sd.Kfz. 251/7 bridging vehicle from an engineer company of the 2nd SS. Behind it is a burned-out M4 medium tank of the 67th Armored Regiment that was destroyed during the nighttime battles.

A 57mm gun crew of the 41st Armored Infantry of the 2nd Armored Division sets up an ambush position.

A motley collection of German artillery lies abandoned around the Roncey school building. To the left is one of the most modern and powerful antitank weapons of the campaign, the 88mm PaK 43, while to the right is a French artillery half-track towing a Soviet 76.2mm F-22 USV field gun, a weapon widely used by the Germans as an antitank gun.

Allied air superiority led the Wehrmacht to pay serious attention to air defense. One of its most effective weapons was the 20mm FlaK 38 mounted on the Sd.Kfz. 7 half-track. This vehicle from the 2nd SS Panzer Division was abandoned in the Roncey pocket and is being inspected by some GIs.

A nighttime attempt to break out of the Roncey pocket failed. At the head of a retreating column from the 2nd SS Panzer Division at the crossroads near Notre-Dame-de-Cenilly was this 150mm Hummel self-propelled gun (named *Clausewitz*) and Sd.Kfz. 251 half-track, followed by about ninety other vehicles and 2,500 Waffen SS troops. It was finally stopped around midnight on 28 July at a roadblock of Company I, 41st Armored Infantry Regiment, 2nd Armored Division. The ensuing traffic jam along the hedgerow-lined road left the remainder of the retreating column exposed to American fire, and a savage battle began in which the column was largely destroyed.

Dry Run, an M26 tractor with M15A1 semi-trailer, is used by the 66th Ordnance Battalion to evacuate a captured Panther Ausf. A. This tractor-trailer combination was popularly called the Dragon Wagon.

This M2 half-track of the 41st Armored Infantry Regiment of the 2nd Armored Division was one of those re-armed with a 37mm antitank gun. However, the large gun shield has been removed, probably because it interfered with the traverse of the weapon in the cramped interior of the half-track. The squad is wearing the distinctive and controversial camouflage battle dress, which was largely discontinued after August 1944.

This Pz.Kpfw. IV Ausf. J from 2nd SS Panzer Division was knocked out by a 37mm gun mounted on an M2 half-track of the 41st Armored Infantry Regiment during fighting for St. Denis-le-Gast on 31 July. A tanker from the supporting 67th Armored Regiment points to a hole in the turret side skirts where the round penetrated.

An M3A1 half-track of the 3rd Armored Division passes through the ruins of Roncey on 1 August. In the wreckage is a destroyed Sd.Kfz. 7 fitted with a quadruple 20mm antiaircraft gun and a 75mm Panzerjäger 38(t) Ausf. M (Sd.Kfz. 138) tank destroyer. The M3A1 half-track is towing a 37mm antitank gun, a weapon inadequate for antitank defense in 1944.

Here, a woman from the town walks past the several wrecked Panzerjäger 38(t) Marder III, showing some of the same wreckage as the previous photo from a different perspective.

Another view of the devastation inside the small town of Roncey following the encirclement battle.

An ordnance team prepares to recover *Destroyer*, an M4 tank of 2nd Armored Division that has overturned after going over a hedgerow at too steep an angle near Canisy during Cobra. Prior to the operation, one out of every five of the division's tanks was fitted with Culin prongs.

A company of M8 75mm howitzer motor carriages from the 3rd Armored Division takes up firing positions along a tree line near Marigny on 28 July. The censor has covered over the front details of the lead vehicle, obscuring the hedgerow cutter on the bow, which was considered a big secret at the time.

This Panther Ausf. A was found knocked out in a hedgerow-lined road outside Coutances on 28 July.

The key road junction at Coutances fell on 28 July to CCB of the 4th Armored Division, which had advanced down the coast against modest opposition. Here, a heavily camouflaged M5A1 light tank passes through the damaged town.

A column of M4 tanks of the 6th Armored Division moves through Coutances on 29 July as they start their race toward Brittany. This was one of two armored divisions of Patton's newly activated U.S. Third Army.

An M4 of the 4th Armored Division passes through Coutances in late July 1944. Both the 4th and 6th Armored Divisions were funneled through the town on the way to Avranches, the gateway to Brittany.

An M3A1 half-track of the 4th Armored Division passes through Coutances in late July 1944.

An M4 (named *Fury*) of the 2nd Armored Division on the move with infantry aboard during Cobra. It is finished in the distinctive First Army camouflage scheme of black over olive drab adopted prior to the start of the offensive.

French townspeople wave enthusiastically as a column from the 4th Armored Division races southward from Coutances in late July. Patton's Third Army pushed down the coastal roads toward Brittany while Bradley's First Army encircled the German panzer formations farther east.

An M31 tank-recovery vehicle recovers an M4 medium tank bogged down on a country lane. To the right is an abandoned German Sd.Kfz. 251 half-track. Although armored divisions were nominally allotted the newer M32 tank-recovery vehicle, many of the older divisions still used the older M31 in Normandy, which was based on the M3 medium tank chassis.

An M3 half-track of the 823rd Tank Destroyer Battalion is seen here towing a 3-inch antitank gun during operations in support of the 30th Infantry Division. The 3-inch antitank gun was used in the towed tank destroyer battalions. Organic antitank companies in the infantry divisions used the 57mm antitank gun through the end of the war.

An M7 105mm howitzer motor carriage towing an M8 armored trailer passes by a cemetery near St. Gilles on 29 July, with the grave of a German SS officer of the 17th SS Panzer Grenadier Division in the foreground. When carrying 105mm ammunition, the M8 trailer could hold forty-two rounds.

A field near Coutances serves as a hasty gravesite for German troops killed in the Normandy fighting. In the background are an overturned Sd.Kfz. 251 half-track to the left and a Pz.Kpfw. IV tank to the right.

A U.S. Army bulldozer pushes a wrecked Pz.Kpfw. IV off the road in the 1st Infantry Division's sector in late July 1944.

An M7 105mm howitzer motor carriage, probably from the 4th Armored Division, leads an armored infantry column through Coutances on 30 July. The crew has rigged a stowage rack on the front holding five oil cans.

An infantry column marches past a pair of M4 Sherman tanks in the ruins of Coutances after the U.S. Army had gained control of the town in late July. The tank to the right is a new M4 105mm howitzer tank that entered production in February 1944. These howitzer tanks were usually deployed in the HQ of tank battalions to provide added fire support.

A jeep and an M4 medium tank of the 6th Armored Division pass through Brehal on 31 July on their way to Brittany. The white triangle on the hull side of the M4 identifies this tank as part of the 68th Tank Battalion, and the tactical number 62 identifies it as part of Company C, which used the numbers 61 to 78.

A column of M4 tanks from the 15th Tank Battalion, 6th Armored Division, tries to negotiate a large crater in the road caused by mines.

Another view of a column from the 6th Armored Division. Led by an M4 tank, it passes through a village on the way to Brittany. The 6th used distinctive white tactical "speed" numbers painted on the hull side for radio communication between their tanks.

An M3A1 half-track of the 6th Armored Division passes through the ruins of Lessay on 28 July.

An M4 medium tank of the 6th moves through the ruins of Lessay on 28 July. This division was attached to Patton's newly activated Third Army.

An M3A1 half-track of the 6th Armored Division passes through Le Repas on 31 July, with a German prisoner of war on the hood of the vehicle.

The clear superiority of the Panther over the Sherman in Normandy led U.S. Army officers to try to develop antidotes. A few captured Panthers were subjected to fire from various types of weapons at a test field near Isigny, trying to determine the Panther's weak spot.

An M7 105mm howitzer motor carriage of Battery B, 22nd Armored Field Artillery Battalion, 4th Armored Division, passes through the ruins of Coutances on 31 July on its way to Brittany. The town of Coutances was shattered by repeated Allied bomber attacks and artillery barrages since it controlled Route N171, the main coastal road south out of Normandy and into Brittany.

An M4 tank of the 8th Tank Battalion, 4th Armored Division, passes through Coutances in pursuit of retreating German forces on 31 July. The 8th heavily camouflaged its tanks with mud and foliage prior to the breakout efforts near Coutances.

Several M4 medium tanks from the 4th Armored Division burn in a field outside Avranches during fighting there on 31 July. The tank in the foreground has suffered an ammunition explosion in the right sponson which has blown the sponson floor down onto the upper run of track. Although the gasoline-powered versions of the Sherman were notorious for their tendency to burn after hit, these early Shermans were more vulnerable to catastrophic ammunition fires.

An M3 half-track of the 146th Armored Signal Company moves across a new bridge laid by divisional engineers of the 6th Armored Division during operations near La Rogue on 31 July. This half-track has been modified with additional radio equipment as can be seen from the many whip antennas. The vehicles in the background are from the division's 25th Armored Engineer Battalion and the divisional headquarters.

An M5A1 (named *Mickey Georgiana*) of the 4th Armored Division in Sartilly on 31 July, possibly of the division's 25th Cavalry Recon Squadron. The cartoon markings were seen on a number of division tanks, most commonly with the 37th Tank Battalion.

No doubt the most feared weapon in the German arsenal was the 88mm FlaK 36 antiaircraft gun, widely used in a secondary antitank role. It was not as common as most GIs, who called almost any antitank gun an 88, seemed to think. The smaller and more versatile 75mm PaK 40 antitank gun destroyed far more Allied tanks in Normandy, but most of its victims were credited to the more celebrated 88. This particular gun was captured by American forces on 31 July.

Heavy firepower was provided by nondivisional M1 8-inch howitzer units like the 105th Field Artillery Battalion seen here, supporting the First Army near Carentilly on 31 July. In contrast to the Wehrmacht, which depended heavily on horse-drawn artillery, American artillery was heavily mechanized, like the this M4 eighteen-ton high-speed tractor towing a howitzer named *Berlin Buster*.

CHAPTER 5

Breakthrough to the Seine

HITLER'S RESPONSE TO THE AMERICAN armored breakout of Operation Cobra was to stage a panzer counteroffensive, dubbed Operation Lüttich. The aim of this operation was to cut off Patton's armored spearhead in Brittany by a panzer drive to the sea. It was a spectacular miscalculation. In reality, the weakened German panzer units no longer had the offensive power to conduct operations of this magnitude in the face of predatory Allied air power. Most of the Germans' panzer strength was located in the British-Canadian sector south of Caen. Moving the panzer force from the Caen sector to the St. Lô sector gravely weakened the German defenses that faced the British and at the same time subjected the panzer force to relentless air attack. Operation Lüttich was stopped cold at Mortain by the U.S. 30th Infantry Division, backed by substantial artillery and air support. With the panzer forces badly beat up, British forces stormed out of the Caen area, and a gigantic pincer began to form around the German army in Normandy near Falaise.

Patton quickly appreciated that the mission to seize Brest in Brittany wasted his forces since the Germans would demolish the port prior to its capture as they had done to Cherbourg. He convinced Omar Bradley, the U.S. First Army's commander, to reorient most of his forces back eastward. His aim was to exploit the catastrophe enveloping the Germans in Normandy and race past their trapped forces toward the Seine River. The British-Canadian pincer aimed at Falaise was slower than anticipated because of determined German resistance, but the U.S. Army was able to charge across France farther to the south, reaching the Seine by the third week of August. The Falaise pocket trapped most of the German forces in France, and even those that escaped had to run the gauntlet a second time to escape across the Seine.

By the third week of August, the northern elements of Patton's Third Army had two infantry divisions supported by the 5th Armored Division on the Seine near Mantes above Paris and had begun crossing the river on 19 August. On the center axis, the 5th Infantry Division and the newly arrived 7th Armored Division aimed for the cathedral city of Chartres and the Paris-Orléans gap. On the southern axis, the XII Corps, including the 4th Armored Division, was operating "deep in Indian country" with hardly any German forces in sight and moving swiftly toward the Champagne region. While little thought had been given to liberating Paris, the City of Lights beckoned.

An M10 3-inch gun motor carriage enters Percy during Operation Cobra on 1 August.

A trio of Sd.Kfz. 251 Ausf. D armored infantry half-tracks knocked out by a Ninth Air Force air strike near Gavray on 1 August.

An all-too-common scene in France in the summer of 1944: a burnt-out column of German vehicles. The armored vehicle is a StuG IV, probably from the 17th SS Panzergrenadier Division.

France's premier armored unit was the 2e Division Blindée (2e DB), commanded by Gen. Philippe Leclerc and attached to the U.S. First Army in Normandy. The French came ashore at Utah Beach starting on 1 August and entered the fighting against the 9th Panzer Division around Argentan on the tenth. Here, an M31 tank-recovery vehicle of the 1/RMT comes ashore from a U.S. Navy LCT.

An M8 75mm howitzer motor carriage of the 2e DB is loaded aboard an LST in the United Kingdom for transit to Normandy in early August 1944 during the transfer of the division to combat.

A French M5 or M9 half-track of the 2e DB stalls out in the surf while coming ashore at Utah Beach in early August. The shield on the side suggests it was in use by an antitank unit to tow the 57mm gun, which had the supplementary splinter shield seen on this vehicle. The M5 and M9 half-tracks were built by International Harvester and were alternatives to the M2 and M3 half-tracks. They were not used by the U.S. Army in the ETO, but were supplied to Lend-Lease Allies such as Britain and France. They are externally indistinguishable but had internal stowage differences.

An M4A2 of the 12e RCC, 2e Division Blindée, lands from an LST at Utah on 2 August. By mid-August, the division was committed in the drive to liberate Paris. Notice the SOMUA name plate on the hull, a reminder of the regiment's use of SOMUA S35 cavalry tanks during the fighting in Tunisia in 1943.

Tarentaise, a French M4A2 of 12e RCC, 2e DB, comes ashore from an LST at Utah on 2 August. The M4A2 was a diesel-powered version of the Sherman and was not regularly used by the U.S. Army. It was mainly produced for Lend-Lease supply to the Soviet Union, but it was also used by the U.S. Marine Corps in the Pacific.

Here, the M4A2 tanks of the 2e DB are parked in a field near Utah Beach, shortly after the division had been landed from England on 2 August. The markings on the hull side of the M4A2s reveal them to belong to the 12e Regiment de Chasseurs d'Afrique (RCA).

The 2e Division Blindée was organized and equipped like an American armored division, but it kept its French unit designations. This is an M3A3 light tank (named *Vexin*) of the 12e RCA, one of the division's three tank battalions.

Field Marshal Günther von Kluge, commander of German forces in the West, attempted to prevent Cobra from spilling over the Vire River by sending the 2nd Panzer Division to Tessy-sur-Vire in late July. The town was finally taken by CCA, 2nd Armored Division, and the 22nd Infantry on 1 August. Some of destroyed German armor left behind included this Flakpanzer 38(t) of Panzer Regiment 3. This was the most common type of German antiaircraft vehicle in Normandy and consisted of a 20mm automatic cannon mounted on a Czech Pz.Kpfw. 38(t) tank chassis.

The Jagdpanther was first encountered in Normandy. This was a tank destroyer version of the Panther tank, but armed with an even more powerful 88mm gun. In Normandy, these served in small numbers with a company from schwere Panzerjäger Abteilung 654 (654th Heavy Tank Destroyer Battalion). As a result, when the first few were captured, they were the source of considerable interest by U.S. Army technical intelligence. This photo was taken by a technical intelligence team of the U.S. First Army.

Another view of a Flakpanzer 38(t) captured by the U.S. Army in Normandy and seen here in an ordnance holding area.

One of the dreaded 88mm flak guns, abandoned during the summer of 1944.

The armored cavalry served a vital role in the exploitation phase of Cobra, racing through gaps in the German rear areas. Here, a patrol from the HQ troop of the 42nd Cavalry Reconnaissance Squadron (Mechanized) with the 2nd Cavalry Group receives a warm welcome in Brehal on the northern approaches to Avranches on 2 August. This unit was popularly called "Patton's Ghosts" and served with the U.S. Third Army during the Normandy and Brittany campaigns.

The M2 half-track was widely used for towing the 57mm antitank gun until the authorized one-and-a-half-ton truck became available. This combination is seen near the cathedral in La Poeles on 2 August.

An M3A1 half-track passes by an abandoned StuG III assault gun during operations near St. German de Tallevende on 3 August. The 17th SS Panzer Grenadier Division and 2nd SS Panzer Division were trapped in the Roncey pocket north of here during Cobra, and this is probably one of the remaining vehicles from the divisions.

A pair of M8 armored cars of Company C, 82nd Reconnaissance Battalion, 2nd Armored Division, pass through the road junction at St. Sever Calvados on 3 August. They have a machine-gun ring-mount field modification so commonly seen in Normandy.

GIs of the 35th Division pass by the wreck of a Pz.Kpfw. IV of Panzer Regiment 3, 2nd Panzer Division, in Pontfarcy on 3 August.

Another Pz.Kpfw. IV of Panzer Regiment 3 of the 2nd Panzer Division knocked out in the fighting near Pontfarcy in early August.

The intensity of the fighting in early August is evident in this view from the town of Juvigny-le-Terte near Mortain on August 2, where a M4 medium tank still smolders after having been hit and a German StuG III assault gun lies opposite.

Some idea of the devastation in the Falaise pocket can be appreciated from this scene with a Pz.Kpfw. IV and a pair of Sd.Kfz. 251 half-tracks.

An M5A1 light tank (named *Doodle Bug*) parked near Chateau Contier on 7 August.

The encirclement of the Falaise pocket in late August left large quantities of heavy equipment abandoned along the roads. Here, a GI looks over the devastation near Chambois, with a 15cm Panzer-werfer 42 artillery multiple rocket launcher in the background.

The Allied armies closed the Falaise pocket at a junction between the Polish, Canadian, and American units near Chambois. The town is littered with equipment, including a wrecked Pz.Kpfw. IV in the foreground.

A Grille self-propelled howitzer abandoned in France. This consisted of the 150mm SiG 33/1 heavy infantry gun mounted on a Czechoslovakian Pz.Kpfw. 38(t) light tank chassis.

An M4A1 (76mm) of the 67th Armored Regiment, 2nd Armored Division, passes through Sever Calvados on 3 August during the Normandy breakout.

An M7 105mm howitzer motor carriage is seen with its howitzer tube in full recoil during the fighting near St. Pois on 3 August. The censor has obliterated the unit crest on the forward side of the vehicle and the Culin hedgerow cutter fitted to the front of the vehicle.

An interior view from an M7 of the 6th Armored Division in France shows the fighting compartment. It provides especially good details of the sights and the lanyard for firing the howitzer along the right side of the gun race.

A Pz.Kpfw. IV abandoned by the roadside during the fighting in the *bocage* in July 1944. Often, abandoned tanks were pushed off roads to clear the path for following vehicles.

Tank destroyer battalions used M20 armored utility cars in their headquarters and for scouting. This one belonged to the 801st Tank Destroyer Battalion, which supported the 4th Infantry Division in Normandy.

An M4 of the 68th Tank Battalion, 6th Armored Division, passes through the heavily damaged town of Avranches on 4 August during the Cobra breakout. Avranches was the gateway from Normandy into Brittany, and so it saw heavy traffic in early August as the Third Army moved westward.

A jeep from the medical detachment of the 704th Tank Destroyer Battalion is parked next to a Flakpanzer 38(t) in France in the summer of 1944. This battalion was attached to the 4th Armored Division.

The Germans threw the fresh 9th Panzer Division into Normandy in the hopes of holding open the Falaise gap. It was beat up in several days of hard fighting on the southern side of the Falaise area by the U.S. 5th Armored Division and the French 2e Division Blindée. This Panther of II/Panzer Regiment 33, 9th Panzer Division, was knocked out by artillery of the 5th Armored Division on Rue de la Poterie in Argentan during the fighting there.

Another view of the Panther knocked out in Argentan with GIs sitting nearby on a break.

The 2nd Armored Division entered Barenton on the way to Domfront on 7 August. This is an M4A1 (76mm) of the 66th Armored Regiment, one of fifty-one of these new tanks received by the division in the days before the start of Cobra.

An M4A1 fitted with an M1 bulldozer blade is used to clean up debris in a French town. The heavy air bombardment that preceded Cobra caused havoc to French towns in its path, and the bulldozers were instrumental in clearing roads for following waves of troops.

An armored bulldozer is used to clear the streets in the town of Vire on 8 August.

Obsolete French tanks like this Renault FT were used by German occupation units in France, often times for security duty such as airbase patrols. This example was photographed in Normandy on 7 August 1944.

A wrecked German Sd.Kfz. 251 half-track on 8 August. This is an unusual variant, apparently armed with a 20mm automatic cannon.

A relatively rare example of one of the older Panther Ausf. D captured by the U.S. 5th Armored Division in the summer of 1944. Few of this version were encountered by the U.S. Army in France, the Ausf. A being more common. Paradoxically, the Ausf D. version was the earlier of the two types, being the version which saw the type's combat debut in the summer of 1943 at Kursk on the Russian front.

A camouflaged M4 105mm assault gun of the 8th Tank Battalion, 4th Armored Division, passes through Avranches on its way into Brittany in early August. The 4th and 6th Armored Divisions were the spearheads of the Third Army in its record-breaking drive into Brittany in mid-August.

The combat debut of the M18 in the ETO was with Patton's Third Army in July. This was one of the first M18 tank destroyers knocked out, the vehicle of Sgt. Roger Turcan of Company A, 704th Tank Destroyer Battalion, 4th Armored Division. While advancing north of Rennes in early August, Turcan's vehicle was engaged by an emplaced German antitank gun, which hit the M18 no fewer than seven times, killing three of the crew. Turcan remained with the vehicle, loading and firing the gun until he ran out of ammunition. He was later decorated with the Silver Star for his bravery. This photo highlights the vulnerability of the M18 because of its very thin armor.

Laxative, an M8 75mm howitzer motor carriage of a reconnaissance company of the 2nd Armored Division, moves forward near an M4A1 (76mm) during the fighting near Barenton on 9 August.

Among the Allied units equipped with the M10 3-inch gun motor carriage was the French 2e DB, which played a central role in the liberation of Paris in August. Here, the crew of an M10 (named *Le Malin*, or "The Wag") of the 3rd Platoon, 2nd Squadron, Regiment Blindée de Fusiliers Marins (Naval Infantry Armored Regiment), take care of stowage on the vehicle before moving out. Although not evident in this view, crews of this unit, drawn mainly from French Navy volunteers, often wore the distinctive French naval cap rather than French army headgear.

A detail view of *Laxative* shows additional details of the vehicle, including its Culin hedgerow cutter and its tactical markings. This photo was also taken near Barenton on 9 August.

Another view of the often-photographed *Laxative*, seen at a later stage of the war with some changes in its markings, such as the over-painting of its Normandy tactical numbers.

The crew of an M18 76mm gun motor carriage (named *Bataan*) of the 603rd Tank Destroyer Battalion loads ammunition for a fire mission near Brest on 12 August. The port was enveloped in August, but the German garrison held out into September, leading to a costly siege.

The crew of an M7 105mm howitzer motor carriage of the 83rd Armored Field Artillery Battalion, 6th Armored Division, swabs out the barrel during the fighting for Brest on the Breton Peninsula on 13 August. Most self-propelled guns carried a large camouflage net to provide cover when used from static positions for long periods of time. The seaport at Brest was the main headquarters of the German Atlantic fleet and had been heavily fortified to prevent its capture by Allied forces.

An M5A1 of CCA, 6th Armored Division, passes through the town square of Rostrenen in Brittany on the approach to Brest. In the background is a memorial to the fallen soldiers of the First World War.

A column of M4 medium tanks of the 3rd Platoon, Company B, 8th Tank Battalion, 4th Armored Division, passes through the Avranches area on the way into Brittany in early August. The 8th Tank Battalion made much more extensive use of camouflage than the division's other two tank battalions.

An M3 half-track serves as the tractor for a towed 3-inch antitank gun, seen here near the Citadel in the port of St. Malo in Brittany in August 1944. The M2 half-track was nominally authorized for towing the 3-inch antitank gun, though M3 half-tracks were sometimes substituted.

A 3-inch antitank gun of the 801st Tank Destroyer Battalion being towed by a half-track through a French town in August while supporting the 4th Infantry Division.

An M4 tank fitted with a T1 Culin hedgerow cutter moves through Lambezelec on the outskirts of Brest in August. It is painted in the black-over-olive-drab camouflage introduced by the U.S. First Army in late July 1944.

A well-camouflaged M10 3-inch gun motor carriage of the 644th Tank Destroyer Battalion passes by a farm cart during the operations near Brest. There were three self-propelled tank-destroyer battalions active in the Brittany campaign: the 603rd, 644th, and 705th, the first two using the M10 and the last using the M18 76mm gun motor carriage.

Hitler attempted to smash Patton's race into Brittany by cutting off American forces with a dash to Avranches and the sea. The ensuing Operation Lüttich led to heavy losses in the attacking German panzer formations. Here, a GI inspects a wrecked German Sd.Kfz. 251 Ausf. D half-track near Mortain on 12 August. This was the standard armored troop carrier of the panzer-grenadier regiments in Normandy. German units heavily camouflaged their armored vehicles with tree branches in hopes of avoiding notice by roving Allied fighter bombers.

One of the German Sd.Kfz. 251 armored half-tracks knocked out in the Mortain fighting. This is an Sd.Kfz. 251/9 version, an assault-gun type fitted with a short 75mm howitzer for close infantry support. The damage was probably caused by a direct artillery hit.

French civilians returning to their homes in Villedieu-les-Bailleul inspect a derelict Panther Ausf. A tank knocked out during the Mortain battle.

Operation Lüttich struck the 30th Infantry Division near Mortain but was unable to make any significant penetrations into the infantry defenses. This is a panzer-grenadier column knocked out during the fighting, with an Sd.Kfz. 251 Ausf. D evident at the rear.

A 57mm gun of the 1st Battalion, 39th Infantry, 9th Division, is camouflaged behind wooden debris during the fighting around Cherence le Roussel on 6 August. The battalion received a Distinguished Unit Citation for its defensive actions against the Germans' Mortain attacks.

A camouflaged 3-inch gun in its defensive position during the fighting in northern France on 19 August. The inadequate performance of the 3-inch gun against the German Panther, as well as its lack of mobility, led American commanders in Europe to insist that it be replaced by a 90mm gun as soon as possible.

An M4 medium tank of the 10th Tank Battalion, 5th Armored Division, on the southern fringe of the Falaise pocket on 12 August during the fighting near Habay-la-Neuve.

An Sd.Kfz. 251 Ausf. D is enveloped in flames after a tank-gun hit on the hull front. This German column was hit near Carrouges on 13 August and is probably one of the units of the 9th Panzer Division that fought against the 5th Armored Division near the Foret d'Ecouves in a forlorn attempt to relieve the Falaise pocket.

The arrival of the 9th Panzer Division near Alecon did little to stem the tide of the American advance. Committed piecemeal, it was ground up in several days of fighting with the French 2e DB and the U.S. 5th Armored Division. Here, one of the unit's Panther Ausf. A tanks is recovered by the French 2e DB.

GIs inspect a Panther Ausf. A of I./Panzer Regiment 33, 9th Panzer Division, knocked out on the road between Argentan and Chambois during the fighting in August.

A Pz.Kpfw. IV of the 9th Panzer Division heavily draped with track for extra armored protection, abandoned in Sees in late August during the fighting with the 5th Armored Division.

The 350th Ordnance Battalion, located on the Normandy coast near Isigny, is seen here preparing new tanks to dispatch to units on 12 August. This includes the first batch of the new M4A3 (76mm), which saw its combat debut with the French 2e Division Blindée in the Paris area in the third week of August.

French civilians in the town of Chavisne welcome the crew of an M4 tank with M1 dozer of the 3rd Armored Division on 13 August.

A burnt-out Panther tank pushed off the road somewhere in France on 16 August.

An M8 75mm howitzer motor carriage of the 3rd Armored Division is greeted by the townspeople of Javron as it passes by a statue of Joan of Arc near the town church. It is an early example of the practice of placing sand bags on the glacis plate for additional protection.

The burned-out hulk of an M8 light armored car is inspected by curious French townspeople as it rests in the town square of Briey on 14 August. These armored cars were used by cavalry reconnaissance squadrons and so took on the dangerous task of probing German defense in the vanguard of the attack.

GIs play a game of cards in Ferte de Mace on 14 August. Behind them is an abandoned Flakpanzer 38(t). This was one of the more common types of German antiaircraft armored vehicles seen in the Normandy campaign, consisting of a 20mm antiaircraft gun on a Pz.Kpfw. 38(t) chassis.

An M5A1 (named *Flathead*) from the 2nd Armored Division in operation near Domfront on 14 August as the U.S. First Army began its surge toward the Seine.

As the Falaise pocket became more constricted, it became a shooting gallery for neighboring Allied units. This Sd.Kfz. 250 armored half-track of the reconnaissance battalion of the 2nd Panzer Division was one of a column of vehicles ambushed by M10 3-inch gun motor carriages of the 813th Tank Destroyer Battalion, which was supporting the attack of the 79th Division near St. Aubin d'Appenai on 14 August.

Troops of the 818th Tank Destroyer Battalion inspect a burning Sd.Kfz. 250 knocked out near Aubin d'Appennai on 14 August.

Another view of the 2nd Panzer Division column, this time an Sd.Kfz. 251 Ausf. D half-track.

A trio of destroyed German Sd.Kfz. 250 light armored half-tracks of the 1st SS Panzer Division by the roadside.

This Pz.Kpfw. IV was found in the Falaise pocket in August. The tactical number is not common and may indicate a tank assigned to the divisional artillery regiment.

A 2nd Panzer Division Panther Ausf. A is examined by U.S. troops after its capture in August. The division's characteristic trident emblem is painted on the turret side in front of the tactical numbers.

A GI inspects a disabled 105mm Wespe self-propelled howitzer near Morteaux on 19 August. This was the German equivalent of the American M7 105mm howitzer motor carriage and consisted of a 105mm howitzer on the chassis of the Pz.Kpfw. II light tank.

In a scene typical of the fighting in the last two weeks of August, an M4A1 (76mm) tank races past a derelict German motorized column. The weakness of the Wehrmacht in the Paris-Orleans gap and the mobility of the U.S. Army overwhelmed the defenses in front of Paris.

An M4A1 dozer tank is used to clean up the ruins in Lonlay-L'Abbaye on 15 August during the pursuit of the German army toward Paris. To the right behind the tank, an M31 armored recovery vehicle can be seen.

The German First Army had very modest resources when instructed by Hitler to block the Orleans gap from Patton's advance. At the time, it had little more than security units with second-rate equipment to take on this impossible task. This 1940-vintage SOMUA S35 tank was typical of the captured French tanks used by these units, in this case with the panzer company of Security Regiment 1010, lost while defending Montargis against the U.S. 5th Infantry Division in August.

An M31 recovery vehicle is waved forward to pull the burning wreck of a German SOMUA S35 tank out of the road from the same improvised roadblock seen in the previous photo.

An M4 tank of the 5th Armored Division passes by an abandoned 75mm PaK 40 antitank gun during the fighting in Dreux on 16 August, part of the Third Army's advance on the cathedral cities of Chartres and Orleans.

During the exploitation phase that followed Operation Cobra, the U.S. Army began committing fresh armor into the battle. Here, tanks of the 31st Tank Battalion, 7th Armored Division, move forward near Chartres on 16 August. The M4A1 medium on the left (named *Battlin' Bitch*) is fitted with the Cullin hedgerow cutter. The tank on the right is an M4 105mm assault gun, a relatively new type that appeared in Normandy in July.

Following the capture of the cathedral city of Chartres, the commander of the 7th Armored Division, Maj. Gen. Lindsay Silvester, drives to the town hall in his M8 armored car to the enthusiastic cheers of the local citizens.

A close-up of Major General Sylvester of the 7th Armored Division in his M8 light armored car in Chartres on 16 August.

Tanks of the 7th Armored Division are seen massed in a field outside Chartres on 17 August prior to moving eastward.

Another scene of a 7th Armored Division bivouac outside Chartres, with the cathedral barely visible in the background, on 18 August. In the center of the photo is an M31B1 tank-recovery vehicle, which was based on the hull of the obsolete M3A3 Lee medium tank.

On 23 August, Gen. Charles DeGaulle visited the recently liberated city of Chartres, and a variety of local dignitaries are seen here at the ceremony. In the background is a Hotchkiss H-39 light tank, first used by the French in the 1940 campaign, captured and re-used by a German unit on occupation duty in France, then recaptured and used by the French FFI resistance forces in the summer of 1944.

A ten-ton wrecker lifts the Wright-Continental R-975 Whirlwind radial engine from the engine compartment of an M4 medium tank of the 2nd Armored Division in a repair yard near Le Teilleul on 16 August.

Orleans fell to an improvised task force based on mixed elements of the 4th Armored Division and the 35th Division on 16 August. Here, an M10 tank destroyer fires on German troops on the opposite bank of the Loire River with the cathedral in the background.

An M10 3-inch gun motor carriage in Dreux, a city on the western approaches of Paris, on 17 August. This vehicle has its tactical numbers on the hull side: the company letter (C) and the vehicle number (32).

A well-camouflaged M16, probably a Patterson conversion, of the 436th Anti-Aircraft Artillery Automatic-Weapons Battalion (Mobile) is seen near St. Denis on 17 August, with its nickname, *Nazi-Nemesis*, painted on the front armored shield.

A late-production M10 3-inch gun motor carriage crosses a treadway pontoon bridge over the Seine in late August during the race across France. Patton's Third Army first crossed the Seine south of Paris on the night of 19 August, setting the stage for the liberation of Paris.

An M4A1 from the Third Army crosses the Seine on a treadway pontoon bridge on 26 August. The army censor has obliterated the Culin hedgerow device on the front of the tank.

The crew of an M7 105mm howitzer motor carriage loads 105mm ammunition during a lull in the fighting. This howitzer used a semi-fixed round with a conventional brass propellant casing that could be easily removed to change charge increments to adjust the range if necessary. The typical high-explosive round weighed forty-two pounds.

An M7 105mm howitzer motor carriage takes part in a fire mission on 20 August near Avet. This is a 1944 late-production type with the factory sand skirts, new suspension, and other late features, such as the basket on the rear sponson box.

A group of M7 105mm howitzer motor carriages from an American armored division awaits further orders in the rolling countryside of northern France.

An M10 3-inch gun motor carriage and M5A1 light tank sit at a crossroads in a French village during Cobra. The M10 is still fitted with the wading trunk that enabled it to land from offshore weeks earlier.

A pair of M10 3-inch gun motor carriages moves across a stream in central France in August 1944. Notice that the lead vehicle is still fitted with Culin hedgerow cutters on the transmission housing. In many cases, these were removed after Cobra because of the excess weight and strain on the front suspension.

A demolished Pz.Kpfw. IV with its engine compartment doors open. It is fitted with triple smoke grenade dischargers on either side of the turret front.

The crews of Company B, 759th Tank Battalion, take a rest in the ruins of Montebourg in August. This was the only separate tank battalion in the ETO to be configured in the rare 1943 light tank battalion configuration, with M5A1 tanks in all four companies.

Following the battle for France, the U.S. Army policed up a large number of abandoned German armored vehicles for disposal and technical exploitation, many at a large holding area near Isigny. This photo shows a Hotchkiss H-39, a light truck, and an antiaircraft searchlight. Curiously enough, some of the French tanks that were captured in good condition were recycled and issued to French resistance units that were used to lay siege to German garrisons in isolated ports along the Atlantic coast later in 1944.

A Panther knocked out by the 704th Tank Destroyer Battalion near Raids during August. This unit was equipped with the new M18 76mm gun motor carriage and was attached to the 4th Armored Division.

Another view of a Panther knocked out in Raids by the 704th Tank Battalion while defending a key road junction.

During August, Patton's Third Army raced across France as the Wehrmacht retreated in disorder. Here, on 21 August, an M4 tank of the 8th Tank Battalion, 4th Armored Division, fires on German troops across the Marne River trying to destroy one of its bridges.

Another view of the scene as tanks of the 8th Tank Battalion engage German troops over the Marne.

An M4 medium tank passes by an abandoned Wehrmacht medical evacuation cart during the operations on the approaches to the Seine in August.

An M29 Weasel of the 904th Field Artillery Battalion, 79th Division, crossing a treadway bridge over the Seine near Mantes during the fighting for the Seine bridgehead north of Paris on 22 August. The vehicle is heavily loaded down with gear and the roll of communication wire suggests that this vehicle was used to lay wire between the batteries.

An M10 3-inch gun motor carriage company of the 818th Tank Destroyer Battalion moves forward through Fountainebleu while supporting the 11th Infantry, 5th Infantry Division, in the outskirts of Paris on 23 August. The infantry in the center are from a bazooka team, with two GIs carrying additional rockets in a special sling carrier.

A wary group of soldiers from the 11th Infantry Regiment accompany M10 3-inch gun motor carriages during the advance through Fountainebleu on 23 August. The bazooka man to the left is the same man seen in the previous photo.

A scene farther up the road as an M10 of the 818th Tank Destroyer Battalion begins to engage German targets across the nearby Seine.

An M4A1 medium tank carrying an infantry team advances past a disabled German artillery half-track during the operations by the 2nd Armored Division along the Seine north of Paris around Venon on 23 August.

A 2nd Armored Division M4A1 (76mm) in action around Venon on 23 August.

A column of M4 tanks passes a burning farmhouse near Venon during the river-crossing operations along the Seine on 23 August.

CHAPTER 6

On to Paris!

A POPULAR INSURRECTION BROKE OUT in Paris on Saturday, 19 August 1944, led by the FFI resistance groups (*Forces Françaises de l'Intérieur*). The U.S. Army had not originally planned to liberate the city since it would be a drain on resources. At a meeting on 22 August, Bradley and Eisenhower agreed that the situation in Paris was getting out of hand and that they would have to intervene regardless of previous planning. Eisenhower had already promised Gen. Charles DeGaulle, head of the Free French forces, that Gen. Jacques Leclerc's 2e Division Blindee (2e DB, or the French 2nd Armored Division) would be given the honor. In view of Leclerc's penchant for independent action, Bradley wanted it reinforced. The reliable and experienced 4th Infantry Division was assigned the Paris mission, supported by the 70th Tank Battalion.

The advance began on the morning of Wednesday, 24 August. Although the German forces in the area were not crack troops, the approach route was heavily urbanized, forcing motorized units to stick to the roads. Most of the main roads were covered by flak batteries protected by small detachments of troops. Leclerc was exasperated by the delays caused by the German defenses throughout Thursday, and he insisted that at least some elements of the 2e DB reach the city center that day. In the early evening, he dispatched a small detachment into the city consisting of three tanks, six half-tracks with elements of two infantry platoons, and some miscellaneous engineer vehicles. Shortly after dark, the massive bells at Notre-Dame began to chime to announce their arrival, soon repeated by all the church bells in central Paris. The German commander of the Paris garrison phoned Berlin and held the telephone up to the sound of ringing bells: "The Allies have arrived." The Paris garrison had been starved of troops to support the Normandy front, and the battle for Paris was quickly over on 25 August 1944.

With the Germans in full retreat, Gen. Phillipe Leclerc won approval from Eisenhower to dispatch the French 2e Division Blindée (2e DB) to liberate Paris. French civilians cheers as an M20 armored utility vehicle of the 2e DB heads to Paris.

French tankers of the 2e DB prepare their Shermans to march on Paris. The M4A2 seen here is No. 30, *Savoie*, of the command platoon of 2/12 Regiment des Chasseurs d'Afrique (12e RCA) commanded by Lieutenant Rives-Henry. It was destroyed in combat a few days later on 11 August.

An M4A2 medium tank of the 12e RCA (No. 26, *Iseran*), commanded by Junior Lieutenant Martin, moving out toward Paris. This unit had served on SOMUA S35 cavalry tanks in Tunisia in the spring of 1943, and many of its Shermans had the SOMUA plaque affixed to the front headlight guard as seen here.

M4A2 No. 25 (named *Morvan*) of the 12e RCA, commanded by Lieutenant Douboster, heads out for Paris while an MP looks on. This tank was destroyed in combat a month later on 12 September.

M4A2 No. 22 (named *Vivarais*) of the 12e RCA, commanded by Junior Lieutenant Guillot, on its way to Paris. This tank was lost to a mine on 15 April 1945.

The crews of a number of M10 3-inch gun motor carriages prepare their vehicles to move on Paris. They belonged to the RBFM (Armored Regiment of Naval Infantry) of the 2e DB, which had been recruited from French sailors, which is why they wear the French naval cap.

The tank destroyers of the RBFM move out toward Paris. This unit saw a great deal of fighting in central Paris on 24–25 August, including some of the best-known engagements in the center of the city around Place de la Concorde and the Arc de Triomphe.

An M8 75mm howitzer motor carriage of the 2e DB heads through a French town on the way to Paris during the third week of August.

The 2e DB encountered the strongest German resistance along the southern route into the city on 23 August. This M8 light armored car is seen overlooking a German street barricade in Antony in the Paris suburbs.

Here, on 24 August, a tank column of M4A2 medium tanks of Bilotte's GTV battle group fights its way through Antony, a suburb of Paris about five miles to the southwest.

Another view of the column of M4A2 tanks of the GTV battle group in Antony on the southern approaches to Paris.

As German resistance faded after the fighting on 24 August, the FFI captured several tanks from the Germans, including this Renault R-35.

An M4A2 tank from General Bilotte's combat command advances along the tree-lined banks of the Seine through an improvised barricade on 24 August.

An M4 tank of the 2e DB engages German snipers on a street in Paris on 25 August, assisted by local police and FFI members.

The tanks of Panzer Kompanie Paris were amongst the most feared weapons available to the German defenders since the FFI had few weapons effective against them, except for Molotov cocktails. The capture of these tanks was a major prize, and this shows one of the company's Renault R-40 tanks taken in the final days of the fighting and used during the fighting near the German headquarters in the Hotel Majestic.

A crowd gathers near the German headquarters in the Hotel Majestic, littered with wrecked equipment. The burned-out vehicle in the left background was a 47mm Panzerjäger based on a Renault R-35 chassis that was knocked out by a French Sherman. In the foreground is a Renault R-40 of Panzer Kompanie Paris, and in the upper right is a Renault R-35.

A dramatic moment as M4A2 tanks of Leclerc's 2e Division Blindée enter Paris along Avenue Victor Hugo on 25 August.

The Luxembourg Palace was one of a number of buildings used by the German garrison as headquarters. It is seen here on the afternoon of 25 August after the fighting, with an abandoned Renault FT tank in the courtyard. These old French World War I tanks were widely used by the Germans in France for security duties.

This Panther tank was knocked out on the Place de la Concorde in the heart of Paris by a 76mm round from an M4A3 (named *Champagne*) of the 12e RCA.

A French M5 or M9 half-track patrols through Paris on 25 August, hunting down German stragglers from the Paris garrison.

A French M10 3-inch gun motor carriage (named *Corsaire*) of the RBFM takes part in the fighting near Rue de Fleurus on the afternoon of 25 August.

An M3A3 light tank of the 4/501 RCC guards the entrance to the French Senate courtyard during the fighting in this area on the afternoon of 25 August.

Among the more obscure German armored vehicles captured in Paris was this pair of 20mm FlaK 38's mounted on an armored version of the Sd.Kfz. 11 half-track and found in the Senate garden.

An M10 (named *Mameluk*) of the RBFM is stationed at a barricade while French civilians talk to the crew on 25 August.

While the fighting went on in Paris, there was extensive fighting on either side of the city. This column of M4 tanks of Company C, 17th Tank Battalion, 7th Armored Division, is seen in action near Melun to the southwest of Paris on 22 August, where Patton's Third Army was expanding its bridgeheads over the Seine.

An M8 75mm howitzer motor carriage (named *L'Arquebuse*) of the 12e Cuirassiers is swarmed by civilians while taking part in the fighting near the Luxembourg gardens, one of the last German strongholds in the city.

By the afternoon of 25 August, central Paris had largely returned to calm. Here, a column from the RBFM takes a break along one of the city streets.

A column of mechanized infantry of the RMT (March Regiment of Chad) of the 2e DB heads down the Champs d'Elysees from the Arc de Triomphe with an FFI automobile leading the way.

An M5 or M9 half-track (named *Neuve*) of 9/III RMT heads down the Champs d'Elysee with the Arc de Triomphe in the background.

A policeman on a bicycle is followed by the first wave of the parade with a patrol of M3A3 light tanks of the security platoon of the GTL battle group at the fore, preceded by a camera truck.

The lead wave of the parade exits from Avenue Champs d'Elysee on to the Place de la Concorde with the M3A3 light tanks in the fore. These photos were taken by a U.S. Army photographer attached to the Office of War Information.

A jeep followed by an M3A3 light tank (named *Limagne*) of the security platoon of the GTL battle group heads through the joyous crowds during the 26 August parade down the Champs d'Elysee.

When the parade reached the Place de la Concorde, some sporadic shooting broke out in the distance. It remains unclear if this came from German stragglers or trigger-happy and undisciplined resistance members. Here, civilians use the cover of an M3A3 light tank of the guard platoon of the Langlade combat command headquarters.

An M4 medium tank, probably from the 70th Tank Battalion, which was attached to the 4th Infantry Division at the time, in the outskirts of Paris.

The first parade by the 2e DB on 26 August was followed by a U.S. Army parade on 29 August, consisting mainly of the 28th Infantry Division but also including elements of the 5th Armored Division and other units from the Paris vicinity. Here, a group of M8 light armored cars line up in front of the Arc de Triomphe.

The M8 light armored cars take part in the 29 August parade.

An M3A1 half-track (named *Heaven Can Wait*) passes the reviewing stand during the parade.

An M4A1 on the left and M4 on the right take part in the parade. The censor has crossed off the Culin hedgerow cutters, which were still considered top secret at the time.

A Patterson conversion antiaircraft half-track on duty in the Tuilleries gardens in Paris next to the Louvre in late August, shortly after the liberation of Paris.

An M3A1 half-track crosses a treadway pontoon bridge over the Seine on 26 August.

The fast pace of the race to the Seine put a premium on mechanized cavalry to scout ahead of the main force and protect the extended flanks. Here, an M8 light armored car of the 87th Cavalry Reconnaissance Squadron engages a German ambush near Epernay on 27 August after the 7th Armored Division had pushed out of the Melun bridgehead on the Seine.

An M16 antiaircraft half-track moves past a truck column on a French road in late August. The Luftwaffe was unusually active in attacking the Mantes bridgehead area on the Seine north of Paris, leading to a concentration of U.S. First Army antiaircraft units.

A half-track column takes a breather in Saint-Mesme, a town on the north-eastern side of Paris. The leading M3A1 half-track is named *Ruptured Duck*.

An M20 armored utility vehicle leads a column from the 813th Tank Destroyer Battalion of Patton's Third Army in the Nancy region in late August 1944. The M20 was a command and utility version of the better-known M8 light armored car, but without the turret.

An M10 3-inch gun motor carriage of the 813th Tank Destroyer Battalion in France in late August. This vehicle has several interesting technical modifications, including an early example of an armored parapet around the turret opening and a Douglas hedge cutter on the bow.

Another M10 3-inch gun motor carriage from the 813th Tank Destroyer Battalion. As can be seen, units did not uniformly apply field modifications to all their vehicles as this one lacks the hedge cutter and extra armor seen on the previous M10. This particular battalion served in support of the 79th Division at this time.

Yet another variation on the extra fittings on an M10 3-inch gun motor carriage of the 813th. This vehicle has a pair of spare road wheels attached to the glacis plate and also has four metal pipes welded to the lower corners of the superstructure that were used to erect poles to hang camouflage netting over the tank. This feature can be seen earlier in this book on the tank destroyer of another battalion, suggesting it was a feature dreamed up by a Tank Destroyer Group headquarters.

A rear view of an M10 3-inch gun motor carriage of the 813th as it passes the battalion chaplain's jeep. The deep-wading trunk fitted at the rear of the vehicle for the original landing in Normandy has been battered, and the rear panel is missing.

An M31 tank-recovery vehicle of the 813th moving up behind the M10 column in late August.

Infantry from the 5th Infantry Division take cover as an M4 of the 735th Tank Battalion engages a target during the fighting in Montereau on 25 August.

An M4 (named *This Is It*) crosses a treadway pontoon bridge over the Marne River. The original bridge had been demolished by the retreating Germans and can be seen in the background.

This King Tiger (No. 121) of SS schwere Panzer Abteilung 101 (101st SS Heavy Tank Battalion) was abandoned near La Cappele when it ran out of fuel and was spiked by its crew. American units subsequently pushed it off the road, and it flipped over as seen here. It was later recovered and today is part of the panzer collection at Münster.

A King Tiger abandoned by its crew. The U.S. Army encountered the King Tiger in combat for the first time in the Mantes bridgehead sector north of Paris when the 3rd Company, schwere Panzer Abteilung 503 (503rd Heavy Tank Battalion) took part in counterattacks. A small number of abandoned King Tigers of Panzer Kompanie (Fkl) 316 were found around Châteaudun.

A knocked-out StuG III with its crew buried alongside it, photographed by troops of the 83rd Armored Reconnaissance Battalion, 3rd Armored Division, in late August.

Officers of the 110th Infantry, 28th Division, inspect a disabled StuG III on 28 August.

An M3A1 half-track of the 3rd Armored Division near Meaux on 28 August. The large bright-colored cloth panel on the corner of the vehicle is a fluorescent pink or yellow air-identification panel.

An M7 105mm howitzer motor carriage passes through Soissons on 29 August.

An M7 105mm howitzer motor carriage crosses a treadway bridge over the Aisne River near Soissons on 30 August.

An M7 105mm howitzer motor carriage. Each vehicle usually towed a separate trailer with additional ammunition, as seen here.

An M5A1 light tank crests a ridge over the village of Buchet on 31 August, with an armored infantry company on M3 half-tracks forming up in the fields below.

M3A1 half-tracks of Company D, 41st Armored Infantry, 2nd Armored Division, pass through the town of Cantigny on 31 August, site of the famous U.S. Army battle of World War I. The lead vehicle, numbered D-9, has the name *Daring* on the side door.

An M15A1 combination gun motor carriage supporting the 90th Infantry Division in Chateau Thierry, overlooking the Marne River on 31 August. The M15A1 can be distinguished from the earlier M15 by the placement of its .50-caliber machine guns below the 37mm gun rather than above. Four days before, the division crossed the Meuse in the wake of the 7th Armored Division and would face a major German tank counterattack a week later between Landres and Mairy.

A member of the French resistance and several tank crews take cover behind an M4 medium tank of 8th Tank Battalion, 4th Armored Division, on 31 August while the tank tries to stop German troops from destroying a bridge over the Marne near Rashecourt.

By the end of August, the Allies had accumulated a substantial inventory of captured German panzers. This is one of the collection points near Trevieres. The turretless tank to the left is a Renault R-35 light tank that had been converted into a 47mm Panzerjäger tank destroyer but had lost its superstructure at some point. Next to it is one of the Becker conversions for the 21st Panzer Division consisting of Chenillete Lorraine converted to a tank destroyer with a 75mm PaK 40, and beyond it are three Panthers.

This photo from the collection point at Isigny near the Normandy coast shows a couple of Panthers in the foreground, followed by some Pz.Kpfw. IVs behind and some Sd.Kfz. 251 armored half-tracks to the left.

Ordnance troops repair a StuG III at Isigny in August. Although the U.S. Army did not systematically use captured German equipment, the holding areas in Normandy served as a source of vehicles for newly created Free French units based on FFI resistance groups that were assigned to siege duties around hold-out German garrisons in the Atlantic ports such as Royan, St. Nazaire, and La Rochelle.

A close-up of the Isigny yard shows a variety of captured vehicles. In the foreground is a pair of Munitionschlepper UE(f) für Raketenwerfer, a German conversion on captured French UE light artillery tractors which added four Wurfrahmen 40 frames to launch 280mm or 320mm artillery rockets.

Many captured UE armored tractors were used for security tasks, and in the case of this example, an armored compartment has been added to the rear to provide a machine-gun position on the vehicle.

American labor leaders on a goodwill visit to the front sit atop a knocked-out Jagdpanzer IV on 24 August. This is the original version of this tank destroyer with the shorter L/48 gun.

The armored protection of the Panther proved to be something of a shock to the Allies when encountered in the summer of 1944. A series of tests was conducted against captured Panthers to determine the effectiveness of various Allied weapons. This is a photo from one of the reports showing the results of trials against three captured Panthers conducted near Isigny in August.

CHAPTER 7

The Other D-Day: Operation Dragoon

THE INVASION OF SOUTHERN FRANCE on 15 August 1944 is one of the least celebrated but most important combat operations by the Allies in the summer of 1944. The U.S. Army wanted to reduce its commitment to the campaign in Italy and shift as many of these forces to the main battle in France. Likewise, the French First Army, raised and equipped by the U.S. in North Africa, wished to return to participate in the liberation of its homeland rather than be squandered in the Italian stalemate. The resulting 6th Army Group, consisting of the U.S. Seventh Army and the French First Army, was assigned the task of landing on the Riviera coast, capturing the key ports of Marseilles and Toulon, and then advancing up the Rhône Valley to meet up with Patton's forces in Lorraine.

Operation Dragoon succeeded far beyond the wildest dreams of its advocates. The landings were conducted by American infantry divisions backed up by tank and tank destroyer battalions. The French units then conducted a vigorous assault on the port cities of Marseilles and Toulon. The Wehrmacht's Army Group G in southern and central France, weakened by diversions of its meager forces to Italy and Normandy, was quickly overwhelmed by the amphibious landings and forced to withdraw. Instead of the bitter attrition battles of Normandy, Dragoon quickly turned into a headlong retreat by German forces up the Rhône Valley with American and French troops in hot pursuit. In the process of retreat, Army Group G lost more than half its forces—over 150,000 troops—as well as most of its heavy equipment. Besides clearing southern France, this rapid defeat forced the Wehrmacht to abandon central and western France except for a handful of Atlantic ports that Hitler ordered held "to the last man."

In the space of less than four weeks, the majority of France was liberated at very modest cost to Allied forces. The U.S. Army in southern France did not deploy any armored divisions until later in the autumn. The main maneuver force for the 6th Army Group was two French armored divisions, the 1e DB and 5e DB (1st and 5th Armored Divisions). The German army in southern France had shed most of its panzer divisions to reinforce the Normandy front earlier in the summer, but the 11th Panzer Division played a central role in the retreat of Army Group G up the Rhône Valley, frequently acting as a rearguard for the less mobile infantry divisions.

The tanks and other armored vehicles participating in Operation Dragoon were fitted with the 5AITC style of wading stacks, as is seen in this view of U.S. Seventh Army M4 tanks in Italy waiting to board the landing craft.

A pair of M4 tanks and M10 3-inch gun motor carriages along a dock in southern Italy prior to boarding ships on 31 July for Dragoon. The deep-wading trunks are the locally manufactured 5AITC type, which had a noticeable center stiffener on the stacks.

The 6638th Engineer Mine Clearing Company is seen here practicing with specialized equipment intended for the Dragoon landings. The locally built mine scarifier on the front of the M4A4 tank was improvised using an M1 dozer and was based on the T5 mine scarifier design. To the left is a Churchill with small box girder bridge, one of three used by the Gapping Team of Alpha Force in support of the 3rd Infantry Division during the landings. The piping near the M4A4 is M2 demolition snake. This was the only combat use of the British Churchill tank by U.S. troops in the war, though British-manned Churchills were sometimes used to support American formations, especially Churchill flamethrower tanks.

One of the most common defenses on the Var coast was the *Panzerturm*, which consisted of the turret from an obsolete tank, such as this Pz.Kpfw. II, mounted on a concrete foundation.

The Wehrmacht did not have the resources to fortify the Mediterranean coast as extensively as Normandy, and many gun positions were improvised. This is a captured French 75mm mle. 36 antiaircraft gun set up for beach defense on Cavalaire Bay/Beach Alpha Red.

One of the most formidable defenses on the approach to Toulon was the Mauvannes battery of 3./MAA.627 (3rd Battery, 627th Naval Artillery Regiment), which was overwhelmed in a "mad assault" by the French Commandos d'Afrique on 18 August with about fifty of its gun crew killed and a hundred captured. The battery consisted of four turreted 150mm TbKC/36 naval guns in M272 casemates.

The Vieux Port area of Marseilles had been heavily fortified for centuries, with the defenses deepened by the Wehrmacht. This is a Bauform 237 *Panzerturm* bunker using a Pz.Kpfw. II tank turret built at the foot of Fort Saint-Nicolas near the entrance of the harbor.

The Wehrmacht fortified the major ports along the Mediterranean coast, and a typical type of beach defense work was the use of obsolete tank turrets mounted on underground concrete bunkers. This example of a Bauform 235 *Panzerstellung* near the Marseilles dock uses an APX-R turret of the type used on French Renault R-35 and Hotchkiss H-39 tanks.

This is another example of a German Bauform 237 *Panzerstellung* tank bunker in Marseilles, this time using the turret from a Pz.Kpfw. II tank.

The larger SOMUA S35 tank turret was also used in the Marseilles defenses. This turret was armed with a 47mm gun. This photo was taken after the fighting in the city, and the commander's vision cupola has been blown off.

Another example of *Panzerturm* defense in southern France, this time using a surplus Pz.Kpfw. 38(t) turret.

A total of thirty-six M4A1 duplex-drive tanks were used during Dragoon, with the 191st, 753rd, and 756th Tank Battalions. Here, on Alpha Beach near St. Tropez, is an M4A1 DD tank of the 756th Tank Battalion, which was supporting the 3rd Infantry Division. The DD Shermans were used with mixed results at Normandy because of rough sea conditions but had fewer problems in the Mediterranean's calm summer waters.

A pair of M4A1 duplex-drive tanks on the beach in front of an LST during the invasion of southern France on 15 August. This amphibious operation is less well known than the D-Day landings at Normandy as it was not as violently contested by the Germans, who were quite weak on the southern French Mediterranean coast between Toulon and Cannes.

An M4A1 DD tank of the 753rd Tank Battalion, which landed with Camel Force in support of the 36th Division near St. Raphael during Operation Anvil, the landings in southern France, on 1 August.

One of the M4A1 DD amphibious tanks of the 756th Tank Battalion was disabled by a mine on Alpha Yellow after having swum ashore. Troops of the 15th Infantry wait nearby for orders to move forward.

This is an M4 tank of Company B, 756th Tank Battalion, a veteran of the Italian campaign, seen in La Lavandou shortly after the 15 August landings.

An M7 105mm howitzer motor carriage of the U.S. Seventh Army comes ashore in southern France as part of Dragoon. The units of this invasion force came out of Italy and so tended to have older equipment than comparable units of Bradley's First Army in northern France.

An M10 3-inch gun motor carriage of Company C, 601st Tank Destroyer Battalion, covers the beaches on 15 August 1944. This battalion had earlier fought in North Africa, Sicily, and Italy, first equipped with M3 75mm gun motor carriages.

An M10 3-inch gun motor carriage (named *Babs*) of the 636th Tank Destroyer Battalion with a full set of wading trunks comes ashore on the narrow and rock-strewn Green Beach with LST-49 in the background. This beach was dubbed "Quarry Beach" by the 36th Division because of the nearby quarry.

An M15 antiaircraft half-track of the 441st Anti-Aircraft Automatic Weapons Battalion in a defensive position on Alpha Red Beach.

This is an M2 half-track car supporting the 141st Infantry, 36th Infantry Division, on Camel Green Beach near San Raphael on the right flank of the landings in the Frejus Gulf. It is fitted with an improvised mine rack to carry additional mines and is towing a 57mm antitank gun. Many of these units used in Anvil were drawn out of Italy and often had Italian-theater markings and camouflage.

An M15 combination gun motor carriage is landed from an LCT at Alpha Red Beach along Cavalaire Bay on 15 August in support of the 3rd Infantry Division. In front of it is an M8 armored car. The antiaircraft vehicles were put to immediate use, as the beach was later attacked by German Ju 88 bombers.

A T28E1 combination gun motor carriage of the 443rd Anti-Aircraft Artillery Battalion guards St. Raphael air base on 17 August after the landings in the 36th Infantry Division's sector. This old vehicle, the ancestor of the later M15 combination gun motor carriage series, had been in combat in North Africa, Sicily, and Italy before being deployed again in southern France.

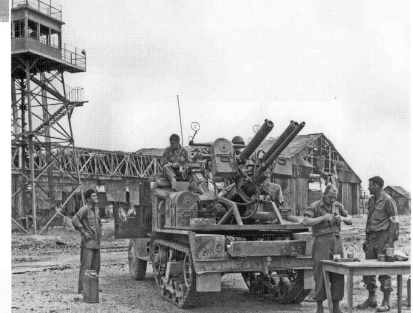

Columns of the 45th Division were motorized by using available trucks as well as attached tank and tank-destroyer battalions. Here, the 45th Division's troops are seen pushing inland on 18 August on the M10 3-inch gun motor carriages of the 645th Tank Destroyer Battalion.

The 117th Cavalry Reconnaissance Squadron was in the vanguard of Task Force Butler and sent north toward Grenoble. Its jeeps and M8 armored cars are seen crossing the Maire River south of Moustiers-Ste-Marie in the Alpes-Maritimes on 18 August.

One of the last remaining T19 105mm howitzer motor carriages in U.S. Army service is seen here in southern France providing fire support for the Seventh Army in late August 1944. By this stage, units in Normandy had completely reequipped with the M7 105mm howitzer motor carriage, and the old T19 was only in service in the Italian theater in dwindling numbers.

A pair of M10 3-inch gun motor carriages of the 601st Tank Destroyer Battalion move over the Durance River near Mirabeau on 20 August while supporting the advance of the 45th Division.

French civilians gawk at an M10 3-inch gun motor carriage knocked out during the fighting in Hyeres in mid-August.

An M4A1 crosses a pontoon bridge over the Durance River in southern France on 25 August as the Dragoon forces spread out from the beachhead. This is an early-production M4A1 as is evident from the M3-style bogies. The forces employed in southern France drew on units from the Mediterranean theater, where the tanks were more dated than reserves in Britain used during the Normandy invasion.

An M4A1 from the 756th Tank Battalion, supporting the 3rd Infantry Division, advances past the burned wreckage of a retreating German column during the advance through the "Corridor of Death" near Montelimar toward the Rhône Valley.

Another view of an M4A1 tank of the 756th Tank Battalion during the push up the Rhône Valley after the Dragoon landings. The camouflage and markings of the Seventh Army units reflected Italian campaign practices, such as the large Allied stars on the turrets.

This Marder III of the 11th Panzer Division was knocked out during the fighting with the U.S. Seventh Army following the landings on the Riviera coast.

A GI looks into the burnt hulk of an M4A1 tank of the 753rd Tank Battalion knocked out in the fighting with the 11th Panzer Division near Grane on 28 August. This is an older Sherman, typical of the veterans of the Italian campaign like the 753rd Tank Battalion.

An M10 3-inch gun motor carriage of the 601st Tank Destroyer Battalion passes through Montelimar on 30 August, along with other elements of the 3rd Division that had been hounding the German retreat. The town is littered with burned-out German trucks, dead horses, and other war debris.

An M8 75mm howitzer motor carriage passes by a burned-out German column in the "Corridor of Death" on the outskirts of Montelimar.

A German StuG III assault gun destroyed in L'Homme d'Armes in southern France.

Past a wrecked Luftwaffe truck, a French M5 half-track moves west from the landing beaches near Ste. Maxime on 20 August.

The French First Army was equipped and trained by the U.S. Army. This is *St. Quentin*, an M4A4 tank of the 2e Cuirassiers, 1e Division Blindée, part of Sudré's CC1, which took part in the liberation of Marseilles.

Tours, an M4A4 of the 4/2e Cuirassiers, 1e Division Blindée, leaving an ordnance area in Ste. Maxime on 16 August after having its waterproofing and wading trunks removed. It saw combat the next day, destroying a German 88mm gun that had destroyed the tank *Tonnere* near Luc.

Vesoul, an M4A2 tank of 2/5e RCA of Sudre's CC1 of the French 1e Division Blindée, fires toward German positions in the Vieux Port area from the plaza in front of the St. Vincent-de-Paul church in Marseilles on 25 August.

An M3A3 light tank of the 1e Division Blindée after the liberation of the port of Toulon in August.

The French First Army took part in the landings in southern France in mid-August, and here, an M8 75mm howitzer motor carriage of the 9 DMI is seen in front of the Palais de Justice in Toulon on 26 August. Behind it are some M3A1 scout cars, a type that had been retired from U.S. Army service but was still widely used in the French units at the time.

The French First Army celebrates liberation day in Marseilles on 29 August with a parade by the 3rd Algerian Division. This overhead view provides good detail of a pair of intermediate-production M7 105mm howitzer motor carriages which are carrying a full load of ammunition in the usual fiberboard tubes.

Following the liberation of the ports, the French divisions began pushing up Route 7 toward Lyon. This is *Belfort*, an M8 75mm assault gun of the 1e Division Blindée, moving through Avignon on 30 August with a column of FFI alongside.

A French M5A1 light tank of the 1e Division Blindée moves through the town of Orgon on 30 August during the pursuit up the Rhône Valley.

In the wake of the fighting, a wrecker truck of the 734th Ordnance Battalion recovers a Pz.Kpfw. III tank from the fields north of Crest. Over a dozen of these obsolete tanks were in use by the 11th Panzer Division as command and forward observer vehicles in the head-quarters company and artillery battalion. Kampfgruppe Thiele (Battle Group Thiele) used some in their skirmishes with the 117th Cavalry in the northern sector of the Montelimar Battle Square.

The 11th Panzer Division attempted to brush back the pursuing U.S. 45th Division, staging a counterattack into the streets of Meximieux in the first days of September. This Panther is one of nine panzers lost in the street fighting.

A pair of M4 tanks of Company B, 756th Tank Battalion, veterans of the Italian campaign, knocked out during the fighting near Vesovi on 12 September as the U.S. Third and Seventh Armies were attempting to link up.

A crew of an M4A1 of the 753rd Tank Battalion enjoys the jubilation of the French crowds as the Seventh Army moves through St. Marie on 16 September. This tank is a veteran of the Italian campaign and carries the characteristic Mediterranean-style shipping code on its bow.

A column of French tanks from the 2e Cuirassiers, 1e Division Blindée, halt in Dijon on 11 September during the race up the Rhône Valley in pursuit of German Army Group G. The last tank in the column is an M4A4 named *St. Raphael* of the 4e Escadron, 2e Cuirassiers.

The symbolic conclusion of Operation Dragoon occurred on 10–12 September when patrols from Patton's Third Army met patrols from the Seventh, marking the link-up of Allied forces from the North Sea to the Mediterranean. To commemorate the event, this photo was staged for the *Stars and Stripes* newspaper in front of the Autun town hall on 13 September, with the crew of a French M20 armored utility car of the 2e Dragons shaking hands with the crew of an M8 light armored car of CCB, 6th Armored Division.

CHAPTER 8

Toward the Reich

BY THE END OF AUGUST 1944, the Allies had liberated Paris and were on the doorstep of Belgium. The U.S. First Army entered Belgium in early September and conducted a fourth great envelopment of German forces in the Mons pocket. The last week of August and the first few weeks of September were dubbed "the void" by German commanders. By mid-September, the U.S. First Army had crossed the Siegfried Line into Germany near Aachen, starting the campaign in Germany.

Eisenhower approved Field Marshal Bernard Montgomery's bold plan to leap-frog to the Rhine plains in northern Germany by seizing a series of key bridges through the Netherlands by means of airborne attacks, code-named Operation Market-Garden. For a moment, it seemed as though the Wehrmacht was on the brink of collapse and that the war might be over by Christmas. But once the German army was back on native soil, its morale improved, and many newly formed units were rushed into combat. The revival of the German army after its crushing summer defeat was dubbed the "Miracle on the Westwall." The Market-Garden operation proved to be too ambitious, and after its failure, Allied momentum soon slowed because of lack of supplies.

Until a major port like Antwerp could be opened, the Allies had to limit their offensive operations. Hitler's main concern was not the British advance in the Netherlands, which could be easily contained because of the terrain, but Patton's advance in Lorraine. Patton's Third Army had made the deepest penetrations of the summer and was on the verge of linking up with the Franco-American 6th Army Group advancing from southern France. Patton's spearheads appeared to be aimed for the Moselle gate, the gateway into the heart of Germany. Germany's newly created panzer brigades were rushed to Lorraine for a massive panzer counterstroke. Instead of a coordinated strike, however, the panzers were committed piecemeal and were ground to bits in a disjointed series of skirmishes. Even though the Lorraine panzer offensive was a complete flop, it represented the most concentrated tank-versus-tank fighting that the U.S. Army encountered until the Battle of the Bulge that winter.

The commander of the 7th Armored Division, Maj. Gen. Lindsay Silvester, is seen in Verdun on 1 September. His armored car is partly covered with chalked markings, a popular activity of French and Belgian civilians during the summer campaign to give thanks for the liberation.

Strangers in a strange land. A group of GIs from the 7th Armored Division have an impromptu lunch on the streets of Verdun on 1 September while curious French onlookers gawk at their unexpected visitors.

An M4 with an infantry squad aboard advances in France on 1 September.

An M4A1 (76mm) of the 3rd Armored Division passes by the burning wreck of a German truck in Aubencheul-au-Bac near Cambrai on its way to the Belgian frontier.

A German armored column retreats through Belgium during the retreat. The vehicle in the foreground is a damaged Sd.Kfz. 250/9 half-track reconnaissance vehicle that is missing its front wheel assembly.

French townspeople swarm over an armored column from the 3rd Armored Division in Mauberge near the Belgian frontier on 2 September. The tank at the right is one of the new M4A1 (76mm). The following day, the division reached Mons in Belgium, setting the stage for the encirclement of the Mons pocket.

An M8 light armored car leads the way over the French-Belgian border on 2 September. The rapid advance into Belgium trapped many German units that had previously escaped encirclement at Falaise and on the Seine.

An M4A1 medium tank, fitted with a Culin hedgerow cutter on the bow, passes through Aubencheil-Aubac near the French-Belgian border on 2 September. The town had been captured only hours before, and a dead German soldier still lies on the pavement.

An M5A1 light tank passes through a town on the French-Belgian border on 2 September. It is fitted with a Culin hedge cutter and sand-bag protection. It carries the typical Allied air-recognition star on the turret roof.

An M8 armored car from C Troop, 113th Cavalry Reconnaissance Squadron (Mechanized), 113th Cavalry Group, conducts a patrol in the Netherlands on 2 September. The vehicle commander is manning the .50-caliber heavy machine gun.

Following the collapse of the German army in France in August, the Allied armies raced into Belgium and the Netherlands. Each cavalry reconnaissance squadron had an assault-gun troop equipped with the M8 75mm howitzer motor carriage, a derivative of the M5A1 light tank with a short-barreled 75mm howitzer in an open-topped turret. Here, a pair of M8 75mm howitzer motor carriages conduct a fire mission on the outskirts of Vic-sur-Aisne in September. The Belgian townspeople frequently chalked greetings on the side of tanks and other armored vehicles after they were liberated, as seen here.

A column of M4 and M4A1 (76mm) tanks of Company I, 33rd Armored Regiment, 3rd Armored Division, advances toward the Belgian village of Ghlin on 3 September.

The 33rd Armored Regiment column reaches the outskirts of Ghlin. This town is in the northwest suburbs of Mons, and the fighting was part of the encirclement of a large number of German troops in the Mons pocket.

Another view of Company I, 33rd Armored Regiment, during the fight against entrenched German infantry in the Mons pocket near Ghlin on 3 September. The tank in the center is one of the M4A1 (76mm) medium tanks received prior to the start of Operation Cobra.

Here, an M4 from the 3rd Armored Division burns in the outskirts of Mons, Belgium, while M5A1 light tanks push ahead in a race for the German border.

Belgians wave to the crew of an M8 light armored car of the 113th Cavalry Group in Rongy, a border town on the French-Belgian frontier south of Tournai.

An M4 from Task Force Taylor enters the Belgian town of Le Cateau on 4 September as part of the V Corps' drive into Belgium that eventually trapped retreating German units in the Mons pocket.

The commander of the VII Corps, Lt. Gen. J. Lawton "Lightning Joe" Collins studies a map while his M20 armored utility vehicle is parked in the town square of Beaumont, Belgium, on 4 September. Collins was one of the most successful American corps commanders during the September fighting, having led the capture of Cherbourg in June and the Cobra breakout in July.

A U.S. First Army mechanized column led by an M3A1 half-track passes through Namur on 5 September while Belgian civilians wave.

This is Panzerzug 32, a German armored train captured on 7 September by French troops in the station of St. Berain-sur-Dheune. This artillery car carries a Chennilette Lorraine converted into a self-propelled howitzer using a Soviet 122mm M30 howitzer.

An M4 tank crosses a treadway pontoon bridge over the Meuse River in Belgium near Namur on 8 September during the rapid advance to the German frontier.

An M18 76mm gun motor carriage (named *Big Gee*) on the streets of Brest, France, on 12 September during the final stages of the siege. While most of the U.S. 12th Army Group was fighting along the German frontier, a force had remained behind in Brittany to conduct the siege of Brest, a critical seaport in Brittany that the Allies hoped to capture. It fell only on 19 September after the Germans had thoroughly demolished the harbor facilities.

An M18 76mm gun motor carriage (*I Don't Want A'*) near a ruined home in the outskirts of Brest on 12 September. The extensive collection of backpacks, bedrolls, and other stowage on the turret was characteristic of the M18, as the vehicle's interior was too cramped to permit much stowage of the crew's equipment. This vehicle is fitted with a Culin hedgerow cutter as well.

A detailed view of the gun tube of an M15A1 combination gun motor carriage. The twin .50-caliber machine guns were usually used to bring the target under fire and range it, after which the more powerful 37mm automatic cannon was engaged.

An M12 155mm gun motor carriage (named *Aiming Post Annie*) fires on targets in Germany from its position in Belgium along the Moselle on 8 September. The M12 was the first American artillery weapon to fire on Germany in 1944.

The crew of an M12 155mm gun motor carriage load a projectile into the breech. The 155mm GPF used a two-part round, with the propellant being loaded as separate bag charges.

By the autumn of 1944, tank destroyer units were increasingly used to support infantry units. Here, infantry of the 3rd Battalion, 22nd Infantry, hitch a ride on an M10 3-inch gun motor carriage during operations near Mabompre, Belgium, on 8 September. This is a late-production M10 with the duckbill turret counterweights. The stub of a wading trunk is still fitted at the vehicle's rear.

Although many American accounts mention encounters with Tigers in 1944, there were in fact very few engagements with this legendary tank since it was so uncommon in the summer and autumn fighting. A few damaged Tiger tanks were captured aboard a transport train near Braines, France, on 8 September by the 468th Anti-Aircraft Artillery Battalion, and one is seen here being inspected by members of the French resistance.

A view of the train at Braines carrying a few Tigers. These were probably from the British sector near Caen, where most of the Tigers operated in the summer of 1944.

The Tigers captured near Braines on 8 September were probably on their way back to Germany for repair and so escaped the encirclement battles at Falaise. In spite of the controversy about the Allied failure to close the Falaise gap, many units that escaped Falaise only ended up becoming trapped during the Seine encirclement in August and the Mons encirclement in early September.

A troop of M8 75mm howitzer motor carriages from the 113th Cavalry Reconnaissance Squadron prepare to conduct a fire mission near Heure-le-Reman, Belgium, on 9 September. The vehicle in the foreground is still fitted with the Culin hedgerow cutter from Operation Cobra in late July.

An M4 medium tank of the 746th Tank Battalion supports the infantry of Company I, 60th Infantry, 9th Infantry Division, during fighting near the Belgian border on 9 September. This tank still has a Culin hedgegrow device on its bow. It was usual U.S. Army practice to attach a separate tank battalion to infantry divisions in combat in 1944, and this battalion stayed with the 9th Division through 1945.

A Dragon Wagon tank-evacuation vehicle recovers an M7 105mm howitzer motor carriage east of Paris on 10 September.

A mechanized column passes through St. Hubert, Belgium, on 9 September, led by a jeep and followed by an M20 armored utility vehicle.

An M4 with M1 dozer is seen clearing a road near Harze, Belgium, on 10 September. Belgian citizens have chalked their names and greetings all over the tank, a popular activity during the liberation of Belgium by Allied forces.

A group of half-tracks from the 3rd Armored Division passes through Theux, Belgium, on 10 September. The lead vehicle is an M4 81mm mortar motor carriage, but it is unusual in that the crew has reversed the side armor panels, and now the access door is on the rear. Note also the bazooka lashed on over the driver's armor plate.

This is a forward-observer tank of the 440th Armored Field Artillery Battalion, 7th Armored Division, which would travel with lead elements of the division and radio back information to the howitzer batteries for fire missions.

In anticipation of encounters with bunkers along the Siegfried Line, elements of the First Army were provided with flamethrowers. Four E4-5 flamethrowers were fitted to M4A1 (76mm) tanks of 70th Tank Battalion on 11 September. These tanks had previously fought in the Belgian campaign, and the chalked inscriptions of Belgian civilians can be seen on the hull side during this training exercise on 13 September. Two of these tanks were temporarily attached to the 741st Tank Battalion and were used to attack a German pillbox three days later. This configuration was found seriously inadequate as the tank had to approach to within twenty-five yards of the pillbox, and even after using up its fuel, the pillbox was not knocked out.

This view looks down into the hatch of an M4A1 (76mm) of the 70th Tank Battalion fitted with the E4-5 flamethrower in place of the front hull machine gun. As can be seen in the upper right, the small flame gun is very difficult to distinguish from the usual machine-gun barrel.

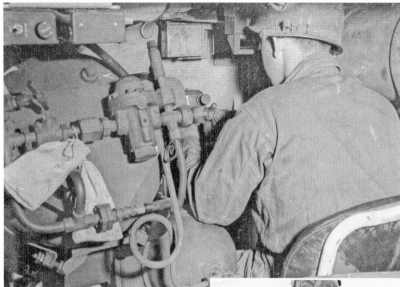

This interior view shows the configuration of the E4-5 flamethrower mounting inside the tank.

A crew from the 70th Tank Battalion tests an E4-5 flamethrower mounted on an M4A3 (76mm) during trials in Belgium.

The 70th Tank Battalion demonstrated the E4-5 flamethrower to several units in September as seen here, and two were attached to the 741st Tank Battalion later for attacks against German pillboxes along the Siegfried Line.

The M6 medium armored car, better known as the Staghound, was a rare case of a mass-produced American armored vehicle that never saw combat service with U.S. units. It was supplied to Britain under Lend-Lease. This is a Canadian Staghound of D Squadron, XII Manitoba Dragoons, in Blankenberge, Belgium, on 11 September. It is fitted with the shrimp netting for camouflage on the turret. NATIONAL ARCHIVES CANADA

An M8 75mm howitzer motor carriage from a divisional cavalry reconnaissance platoon from the 30th Division scouts along a road near Vise, Belgium, on 11 September. The two GIs behind the vehicle are probably from an accompanying infantry unit as cavalrymen were armed with the M1 carbine, not the M1 rifle.

Belgian citizens wave at the crew of an American M3A1 half-track as it passes through Vise on 11 September.

Jubilant Belgians greet the crew of an M2 half-track (named *Alabama*) of the 2nd Armored Division in the town square of Soignies to the northeast of Mons on 12 September.

This M4A3 (76mm) of the 749th Tank Battalion was disabled near Charmes on 12 September during the fighting between the U.S. 79th Division and the German 16th Infantry Division. An antipersonnel mine has gone off under the second bogie assembly, severing the track. This particular version of the Sherman did not begin to appear in any significant numbers in the ETO until September 1944.

An M4A1 (76mm) of the 3rd Armored Division gingerly moves down an embankment on to a treadway bridge erected over pontoons on the Meuse River near Liege, Belgium, on 12 September while local citizens watch. The pontoon bridge was erected alongside the ruins of a bridge demolished by the retreating Germans as can be seen by the abutment to the right. This is the tank of Sgt. Lafayette Pool, who at the time was one of the highest-scoring tank aces in the U.S. Army; he is the standing figure in the photo.

An American bazookaman advances under the watchful eye of an M4A1 (76mm) of the 66th Armored Regiment, 2nd Armored Division, on a road near Haaselt in Belgium on 12 September. On the side of the road is an overturned German staff car left behind during the retreat.

An M2A1 half-track crosses a treadway pontoon bridge over the Meuse in Liege on 12 September as Belgian civilians look on.

A pair of M3A1 half-tracks of the 2nd Armored Division moves through the streets of Winterslag on 14 September. The half-track in the foreground is named *Daring*.

On 13 September, Task Force X of the 3rd Armored Division penetrated the Siegfried Line near Roeten to become the first American troops into Germany. Here, one of the division's M4 tanks drives through some dragon's teeth, the first layer of the Scharnhorst Line.

Elements of Task Force X of the 3rd Armored Division found a gap in the Siegfried Line defense belt. It had been designed to permit German troops to pass through but had not been properly sealed up after the retreat. This is a view two days later on 15 September as one of the unit's M4 dozer tanks moves through the gap in the dragon's teeth.

Another view of a 3rd Armored Division M4 carrying troops of the 36th Armored Infantry Regiment while moving through border defenses near Roeten on 15 September.

An M3A1 half-track leads a column through St. Vith, Belgium, on 13 September with Wehrmacht road signs still evident at the crossroads. The 7th Armored Division would later return to this town during the Ardennes battles in December.

A pair of M10 3-inch gun motor carriages fire on Wehrmacht positions near the German border on 14 September.

On 15 September, after penetrating through the Siegfried Line, the 8th Infantry Regiment began a motorized advance on the Schnee Eifel ridgeline. Supported by M4 tanks of the 735th Tank Battalion, the spearhead came under fire near the town of Roth.

Another view of the same M4 tank of the 735th Tank Battalion inside the town of Roth, with GIs from the 8th Infantry Regiment using the local terrain to provide cover from snipers.

The crew of an M8 light armored car is greeted by friars from a local monastery in Maarland, the Netherlands, in September.

A composite-hull M4 (named *Dodo*) of Company D, 66th Armored Regiment, 2nd Armored Division, crosses a treadway bridge over a stream during operations along the German frontier.

An M12 155mm gun motor carriage in full recoil as the crew braces themselves. This vehicle was widely used during the autumn 1944 campaign for attacking German pillboxes and fortified positions along the Siegfried Line.

A battery of M12 155mm gun motor carriages from the 991st Field Artillery Battalion conducts a fire mission near Bildohen on the approaches to Aachen in September. The vehicles have been driven up improvised ramps to get greater elevation for their guns. The limited elevation of the 155mm gun was one of the main drawbacks of this weapon. The gunner to the right is carrying one of the propellant bag charges for the gun.

The northern flank of the U.S. First Army extended into the Netherlands. Here, an M4A1 (76mm) of Company F, 66th Armored Regiment, 2nd Armored Division, passes through a medieval arch in the town of Valkenberg on 17 September.

A Panther tank of the 2nd Battalion, Panzer Regiment 33, knocked out during the fighting with the U.S. 3rd Armored Division in the Gressenich-Dieplinchen area of the Stolberg corridor on 16 or 17 September.

During mid-September, the U.S. First Army began launching attacks up the Aachen-Stolberg corridor in the hopes of capturing the heavily fortified border city of Aachen. The 9th Infantry Division reached Schevenhütte before being counterattacked by the newly arrived German 12th Infantry Division on 17 September. A task force of the 3rd Armored Division intervened, and a pair of their M4A1 (76mm) tanks is seen in front of St. Josef church on September 22.

To better coordinate fighter-bomber strikes, the 9th Tactical Air Force dispatched pilots like this one to serve as forward observers in tank units to help call in air strikes against key German targets along the Siegfried Line.

One of the shortcomings of the M10 tank destroyer was the lack of overhead roof protection. In September, the 813th Tank Destroyer Battalion had its maintenance personnel attach improvised five-eighth-inch steel folding covers over the turret roof on about half of its M10 tank destroyers in order to provide a measure of protection against small-arms fire. The M10 tank destroyers with the late-production turret had a full kit added, which included folding armored flaps over the rear of the fighting compartment, as seen here.

The two rear panels on the late-production M10 tanks destroyers could be folded forward if necessary for the crew to enter or exit the vehicle.

A burned-out M4A1 tank is recovered by an M25 Dragon Wagon on 22 September. This tank shows the wider mantlet adopted on the M34A1 gun mount on later-production M4A1 tanks.

A pair of M3A1 half-tracks of the 3rd Armored Division in the ruins of Stolberg, Germany, during the initial fighting along the German frontier.

An M3 half-track serves as the platform for a loudspeaker of a psychological warfare unit of the 12th Army Group during a propaganda mission in Eilendorf, Germany, on 23 September. These vehicles would be used for a variety of roles, including warnings to German civilians to evacuate towns that were on the verge of being attacked. They were also used against encircled German garrisons to encourage enemy troops to surrender.

During September, the Allies staged a massive airborne mission called Market-Garden in the Netherlands to capture the Rhine River bridge at Arnhem. Although primarily a British operation, the campaign involved the U.S. Army's two airborne divisions. This is a British Sherman Firefly knocked out in the fighting around Erf while supporting American paratroopers. The Firefly was armed with an extremely potent 17-pounder gun, which had much better antitank performance than the Sherman's usual 75mm gun.

This is a Panther command tank knocked out by a British Firefly supporting U.S. paratroopers near Erf. It is being inspected by one of the paratroopers on 23 September.

The American airborne landings during Market-Garden paved the way for the armored columns of the British 30 Corps. Here, two paratroopers of the U.S. 82nd Airborne Division talk to the crew of a British Stuart light tank of the Sherwood Rangers Yeomanry, 8th Armoured Brigade, which provided armored support in late September and early October.

The various types of "rhino" hedge cutters remained on many tanks into the autumn campaign, like this example of a T1 Culin device on an M4 operating near the Luxembourg frontier in September. It is followed by an M10 tank destroyer.

While Hodges's U.S. First Army was advancing into Belgium, Patton's Third Army was advancing into Lorraine. In one of the more famous incidents in its distinguished combat career, the 4th Armored Division leapfrogged the Moselle River after the Germans had blown up the main bridges by finding a ford over the National Canal near Bayon. The Germans had thought that the canal was impassable to tanks because of the deep mud. The 8th Tank Battalion's crossing of the canal, however, was made possible by the low water level in several sections. This is evident here as several of the barges are left high and dry in the mud. The Sherman exiting the canal is one of the newer M4A3 medium tanks armed with the long 76mm gun. This action was instrumental in capturing the key city of Nancy on the way to the German border.

During a lull in the fighting in Belgium on 30 September, the crew of an M4A1 takes the opportunity to clean the gun barrel.

The crew of an M32 tank-recovery vehicle prepares an impromptu lunch using the tow shackle on the front of the vehicle as an improvised stove during the advance around Nancy in September.

An M4 medium tank fords the Moselle on 15 September during Patton's drive toward the German frontier in Lorraine.

A GI from the 90th Infantry Division inspects some of the German equipment captured by the division during the fighting with Panzer Brigade 106 near Mairy. These are both armed versions of the standard German Hanomog Sd.Kfz. 251 Ausf. D armored infantry half-track. An Sd.Kfz. 251/21 antiaircraft vehicle with a triple MG151 cannon mounting is seen to the left. Panzer Grenadier Battalion 2106 had ten of the Sd.Kfz. 251/9 Stummel assault guns armed with a close-support 75mm howitzer (seen on the right vehicle).

In mid-September, Hitler ordered that four of the new panzer brigades cut off the spearhead of the Third Army east of Nancy in a classic envelopment battle. Panzer Brigade 106, led by the legendary panzer commander Franz Bäke, started off the Lorraine panzer counteroffensive on the night of 7–8 September, attempting to cut off the U.S. 90th Division near Mairy, France. The attack was a shambles, and by the end of the day, the brigade had lost most of its equipment, including 21 of its tanks and tank destroyers, 60 of its Sd.Kfz. 250 and 251 half-tracks, and more than 100 support vehicles. This is one of its Panther Ausf. G tanks abandoned after the fighting and left by the roadside west of Metz for a few weeks for improvised vehicle-recognition training for passing American troops.

American troops inspect a knocked-out column of armor outside Nancy on 10 September during the initial stages of the fighting for Lorraine. These are probably from the 6th Armored Division. The M3A1 half-track has been hit by a high-explosive round, which has caved in the side armor and set the vehicle on fire.

An M3A1 half-track (named *Lucille-B*) of Combat Command B headquarters from the 7th Armored Division. The extra radio antennas typical of a headquarters vehicle are evident here. There is an air-identification panel adjacent to the machine-gun pulpit.

An M3A1 half-track of Combat Command B headquarters of the 7th Armored Division with a pair of German prisoners riding on the fenders.

By mid-September, the Third Army had reached the Moselle and started efforts to make a crossing in force. The northern crossing of the Moselle took place near the town of Dieulouard. Here, an M4 bulldozer tank is used to create a roadway across a narrow tributary of the Moselle on 12 September.

A company of M4 medium tanks from the Third Army provide indirect fire support for operations near the Moselle in September.

An M32 tank-recovery vehicle of the Third Army crosses the Moselle over a pontoon bridge on 13 September.

The second unit to attack in Lorraine was Panzer Brigade 112, which deployed its Panther battalion in Dompaire on the night of 12 September. A combat command of the more experienced French 2e Division Blindée beat up the brigade on 13 September, and after two days of fighting, the brigade had only twenty-one operational tanks out of its original eighty. This Panther was captured by the French intact and for many years was displayed in Paris in front of Les Invalides in central Paris.

Patton's forces surrounded the provincial capital of Lorraine at Nancy, and the 4th Armored Division got over the Moselle near Bayon. Here, on 15 September, in support of the 320th Infantry, which was crossing a nearby canal at the time, an M4A3 medium tank of the 737th Tank Battalion fires on buildings near Dombasle, along the left flank of the advance. This is an early example of the M4A3 in combat in the ETO as the first batches began to arrive in this theater only in August.

An M4A3 medium tank of the 737th Tank Battalion near Dombasle on 15 September 1944.

An M7 105mm howitzer motor carriage of Battery B, 66th Armored Field Artillery Battalion, 4th Armored Division, moves over a treadway bridge during operations along the Moselle in Lorraine. The crew has mounted a shelf over the transmission cover to hold personal gear.

The Wehrmacht responded to the Bayon crossing with a series of counterattacks, including a brief tank attack by Pz.Kpfw. IVs of the 15th Panzer Grenadier Division near Mehoncourt, in which one M4 medium tank of the 8th Tank Battalion was knocked out. It can be seen in the background while a medic tends to a wounded tanker in the foreground.

On 19 September, Panzer Brigade 113 launched an attack against elements of the 4th Armored Division near Arracourt and first ran into the 704th Tank Destroyer Battalion near Rechicourt-la-Petite. A short-range duel in the early-morning fog led to the loss of several Panther Ausf. G's and M18 Hellcat tank destroyers. These are two of the Panthers knocked out during the skirmish.

A Panther Ausf. G of Panzer Brigade 113 knocked out by the 704th Tank Destroyer Battalion during the fighting near Parroy.

In 1945, one of the veterans of the 704th Tank Destroyer Battalion returned to the Arracourt area and photographed several of the Panther tanks still lying abandoned around the battlefield. This is a Panther Ausf. A, most likely belonging to Panzer Brigade 113.

The commander of the 37th Tank Battalion during the Lorraine fighting was Maj. Creighton Abrams, and this was his command tank at the time, named *Thunderbolt V.*

Soldiers of the 704th Tank Destroyer Battalion inspected the inside of this destroyed Panther and found bits of uniform still inside. Additional Panthers can be seen littering the field behind.

Another of the Panther Ausf. G's knocked out in the Arracourt fighting in September near Rechicourt-la-Petite.

An M4 of the 6th Armored Division tries to help pull another M4 out of the mud. One of the most serious shortcomings of the M4 Sherman was its poor floatation in soft soil, mud, and snow. By the late autumn, many Shermans began to be fitted with extended end connectors, sometimes called duck bills, which marginally improved traction in poor conditions.

The crew of an M4 medium tank commanded by Sgt. Timothy Dunn of the 37th Tank Battalion beds down for the night in a field near Chateau Salins to the northeast of Arracourt on the evening of 26 September. The crewman at the front of the tank is removing the Culin hedgerow cutter, no longer needed in the open terrain of Lorraine. This battalion was commanded by Maj. Creighton Abrams, after whom today's M1 Abrams tank is named.

An M18 tank destroyer from the 603rd Tank Destroyer Battalion, CCB, 6th Armored Division, guards the intersection at Rue Carnot in Luneville, facing toward Frambois, on 22 September. Vehicles from this unit took part in the tank fighting in Luneville with Panzer Brigade 111 on 18 September.

Here, an M4 has its transmission serviced in a forested work area during the fighting in Lorraine in late September.

Another view of the Third Army's forested tank workshop, this time with the turret of an M4 removed for servicing the hull. The turret basket can be seen on the ground beyond the tank, while the turret itself is propped up on logs.

Capt. J. F. Brady, commander of A Company, 35th Tank Battalion, 4th Armored Division, shortly after the Arracourt tank battle. This gives a good view of the standard tanker's helmet as well as the tank commander's intertank microphone. The helmet was not armored, so in some units, a normal steel helmet was worn instead when riding outside the tank.

The commander of a heavily camouflaged M5A1 light tank peers through his binoculars. He is wearing the standard tanker's helmet, which was based on a prewar football helmet and so offered no ballistic protection.

CHAPTER 9

The Siegfried Line

IN THE LATE 1930s, Germany had erected a series of fortified defenses called the Westwall. Over the years, the fortification line had fallen into disrepair, and much of the armament had been recycled into the Atlantic Wall fortifications in France. Realizing their vulnerability, the Wehrmacht began to rejuvenate the Westwall in August 1944 and to substantially extend the defenses as the new West-Stellung, better known to the Allies as the Siegfried Line. Most of the fighting in the autumn of 1944 was conducted along this defense line.

By October 1944, the U.S. Army in the ETO had four armies in the field. Bradley's 12th Army Group had three armies operating along the German frontier: Gen. Courtney Hodges's First Army and Gen. William Simpson's Ninth Army north of the Ardennes, with Patton's Third Army to the south, still stalled in the Metz fortifications in France while attempting to reach the German frontier along the Moselle River in Lorraine. Gen. Jacob Devers's 6th Army Group to the south of Patton had two armies in the field, the U.S. Seventh Army and the French First Army, both of which were fighting in Alsace. The 6th Army Group's operations are described in the next chapter while this chapter focuses on the actions by Bradley's 12th Army Group.

After the narrow penetration toward Aachen in September, the U.S. First Army attempted to broaden the penetration of the German defensive belt by a major assault around Ubach on 2–7 October. After the initial infantry attack stalled, the 2nd Armored Division was inserted into the battle, fighting a bitter weeklong battle that brought its forces through the Siegfried Line to the north of Aachen. Aachen finally fell on 21 October 1944 after bitter fighting, the first German city to fall into Allied hands.

With Aachen in American hands, plans for further operations began to take shape. The primary U.S. objective was to reach the Roer River as a first step to crossing the Rhine. The tactical problem in this area was the Roer dams. If the dams were left under German control, any American advance over the Roer would be pointless since the Germans could open up the dams and cut off any advance U.S. forces by flooding the plains behind them. As a result, the capture of the dams became the focus of American attention in October–November 1944. This proved to be far more difficult than anticipated, as the dams were located beyond the heavily wooded Hürtgen Forest.

The attacks toward the dams began in earnest in early October 1944. German infantry resisted with tenacity, and the fighting soon became dominated by deadly artillery barrages from both sides. After many setbacks, the U.S. Army attempted to deploy armor into the Hürtgen Forest in early November when the 28th Division began a second attack on Schmidt, but the terrain did not favor the use of tanks.

In early November 1944, in an attempt to circumvent the bloody quagmire in the Hürtgen Forest, the First and Ninth Armies staged Operation Queen, a combined infantry-tank assault through the industrial region on the edge of the Roer River. The attack began on 16 November with a heavy air bombardment, the heaviest since Operation Cobra in July 1944. Although the bombing suppressed Germany artillery, it did little to soften the German defenses. The U.S. 3rd Armored Division pushed down the Stolberg corridor but was unable to crack

the German defenses. By the beginning of December, the U.S. Army had finally fought its way through the Hürtgen Forest and the fortified towns east of Aachen, finally placing it on the Roer plains.

South of the Ardennes, Patton's Third Army fought its own campaign, largely disconnected from the battles along the Siegfried Line. Instead, Patton faced another fortified zone around the city of Metz, a traditional battleground between France and Germany that had been heavily fortified over the centuries. The fortresses were gradually overcome in bruising infantry battles in November and December, finally putting Patton's forces next to the Siegfried Line in the Saar. Patton planned to launch a major armored drive toward Frankfurt in mid-December—code-named Operation Tink—but events to the north in the Ardennes intervened.

During the attempts by Patton's Third Army to overcome the fortifications around Metz, the 735th Tank Battalion made one of the few uses of the M2 demolition snake in combat. This consisted of up to 400 feet of explosive-packed tubing that was pushed in front of the tank and detonated to blow gaps in minefields. Of the four snakes pushed against Fort Driant on 31 October, three broke up on the approach to the fort, and the last failed immediately short of the fort. This shows the assembly of one of the snakes near Gorz on 2 October.

This shows the appearance of the front end of the M2 demolition snake, which is being welded on near Gorz on 2 October. The front section was intended to make it easier to push the demolition device in front of the tank, but the system proved to be very unwieldy. No snakes were successfully used in the fighting, even though there were experiments in using them to breach dragon's teeth obstacles along the Siegfried Line.

The length of the demolition snake can be seen in this view outside Metz on 2 October as the crew assembles the individual lengths of pipe. The extreme length of the device made it very difficult to use in rough terrain.

This M32B1 of the 712th Tank Battalion has been adapted to carry a length of treadway bridge on the front. This field conversion was undertaken for use in crossing moats protecting the fortresses near Metz during the fighting there in October.

On 6 October, the crew of an M4 tank of the 7th Armored Division helps ordnance repair crews swap out a Continental R975 radial engine. This radial aircraft engine powered both the M4 and M4A1 versions of the Sherman tank.

The M3 half-track was widely used for utility tasks. Here, troops of the 146th Armored Signals Company, 6th Armored Division, lay field telephone wire from the rear of an M3 half-track on 5 October.

A T1E3 Aunt Jemima mine exploder temporarily attached to the 25th Armored Engineer Battalion, 6th Armored Division, rolls down a road near Nancy, France, on 7 October. These types of engineer tanks became more common in the ETO in the autumn of 1944 because of the increasing threat of mines along the heavily fortified German frontier.

An M4 with a T1E3 Aunt Jemima mine exploder of the 25th Armored Engineer Battalion, 6th Armored Division near Nancy. This provides a good view of the rear pusher plate; if the mine-exploder tank became stuck, another tank could be moved up behind it and use this plate to give it a push.

A T1E3 of the 25th Armored Engineer Battalion, 6th Armored Division, crosses the Moselle River on a treadway bridge near Liverdun, France, on 7 October.

On October 8, Mobile Regiment von Fritzchen attempted to push the 30th Division out of Alsdorf. Here, the 117th Infantry has established an antitank defense in the streets of neighboring Schauffenburg using a 3-inch antitank gun of the attached 823rd Tank Destroyer Battalion along with a bazooka team and a .50-caliber heavy machine gun.

An M4 medium tank of the 707th Tank Battalion provides fire support for the 28th Division during fighting against pillboxes of the Siegfried Line along the German frontier east of Elsenborn, Belgium, on 9 October. On the rear hull is painted "Phone," showing where the field telephone is stowed to allow accompanying infantry to communicate with the tank crew. This became an increasingly common fixture on the tanks in separate tank battalions to assist in tank-infantry cooperation in close combat.

In early October, the 2nd Armored Division was used to enlarge a gap in the Westwall around Ubach. An M4 tank of the 3/67th Armored Regiment, 2nd Armored Division, stands guard in an entrenchment on 10 October. Americans having fought through the Siegfried Line, the front turned into a stalemate by early October. This M4 is of the later-production type with the M34A1 gun mount and a full set of hull and turret appliqué armor. The attachment of a spare ten-gallon oil can on the right fender was common practice in some tank units in 1944.

The crew of an M12 155mm gun motor carriage (named *The Babe*) loads a round into the gun during the bombardment of Fort Driant, part of the Metz fortifications, during Patton's difficult campaign around the fortified city on 10 October. Metz was a thorn in Patton's side for most of the autumn of 1944.

The most common method used by the U.S. Army in the ETO for rapidly breaching minefields was the use of mine rollers like this T1E3 near Nancy, seen on 11 October. They were first used in combat by the 6th Armored Division in July, but there was no extensive use until the fall.

Because of shortages of American minefield-breaching equipment, the U.S. Army obtained small numbers of Crab flails from the British. They were first used by a platoon of the 747th Tank Battalion during Operation Cobra in July. Due to the small number available, the U.S. Army frequently requested the assistance of the British 79th Armoured Division to provide flail tank support, and this Crab is in use near Breinig, Germany, on 11 October.

The commander of a new M4A3 tank of the 6th Armored Division observes an air strike by fighter-bombers of the Ninth Air Force on 13 October in eastern France. This particular version of the Sherman tank was powered by a Ford in-line engine in place of the Continental radial used in the M4 and M4A1 versions. It was not widely seen in the ETO until September–October.

The short-range street fighting along the German border in October saw far more extensive use of German Panzerfaust antitank rockets. As a result, American tank units began adding sand bags to the glacis plate of the tank in an attempt to improve protection. This is an M4 of the 3rd Armored Division carrying troops of the 36th Infantry during operations near Stolberg on 14 October.

An M8 75mm howitzer motor carriage crew of Company E, 2nd Cavalry Group, cleans out the barrel of its vehicle during a lull in the fighting near Parroy, France, on 14 October.

The crew of an M8 75mm howitzer motor carriage of Company E, 2nd Cavalry Group, prepares for a fire mission near Parroy on 14 October. The crew is lined up in a chain to pass ammunition from the M10 ammunition trailer to the howitzer crew.

M10 3-inch gun motor carriages of Company A, 634th Tank Destroyer Battalion, fight their way into the outskirts of Aachen on 14 October. Aachen was the first German city entered by Allied forces, and the fighting there was particularly intense. The M10s are late-production types with the improved duckbill turret counterweights. Notice that these vehicle have started to carry sand bags on the glacis plate, an attempt to provide added protection to the thin frontal armor against German Panzerfaust antitank rockets.

A pair of M10 3-inch gun motor carriage tank destroyers of the 634th Tank Destroyer Battalion in action inside Aachen. This battalion was assigned to the 1st "Big Red One" Infantry Division for most of the ETO campaigns.

Infantry from the 1st Infantry Division advance behind an M10 3-inch gun motor carriage of the 634th Tank Destroyer Battalion during the fighting in Aachen.

The M10 3-inch gun motor carriage accompanying the 1st Infantry Division team fires down a street in Aachen on 15 October.

The extent of the damage in Aachen is evident in this view of an M10 of the 634th Tank Destroyer Battalion. The city had suffered from both aerial bombardment and preparatory artillery bombardment, and much of the debris had already been cleared up by German civilians before the actual street fighting began.

An M4 dozer tank of the 745th Tank Battalion breaks an opening at one of the Aachen railroad stations during the fighting for one of the viaducts leading into the city at the start of the Aachen fighting in mid-October.

Catalina Kid, an M4 medium tank of Company C, 745th Tank Battalion, follows the tank dozer through the entrance to the Aachen–Rothe Erde railroad station during the fighting around the city viaduct.

A counterattack by the 3rd Panzer Grenadier Division in Aachen on 15 October is met here by elements of the 26th Infantry, 1st Infantry Division, supported by M4 tanks of the 745th Tank Battalion. The M4 on the left is still fitted with its wading trunk from the landing in Normandy. The 745th Tank Battalion supported the 1st since Normandy, and the tank to the left is still fitted with its rear wading trunk from the landing.

The tactics of the 26th Infantry during the Aachen street fighting used firepower to reduce German defenses. Here, infantrymen of 2/26th Infantry look on while an M4 medium tank of the 745th Tank Battalion blasts away on 15 October.

The armored support elements of the 1st Infantry Division meet at an intersection in Aachen. In the foreground is an M10 3-inch gun motor carriage of the 634th Tank Destroyer Battalion while in front of it is an M4 tank of the 745th Tank Battalion. Barely evident in the upper left is one of the new M4A3E2 assault tanks, a newly arrived type of Sherman with added armor and specifically intended for fighting against fortified objectives.

Another view of the M10 tank destroyers and M4 medium tanks supporting the 26th Infantry, 1st Infantry Division, during the fighting around one of the city viaducts. A bulldozer has been brought in to help clear up rubble.

An M2A1 half-track car attached to an antitank company brings a 57mm antitank gun forward during the bitter street fighting in Aachen on 15 October. The 57mm gun was an American copy of the British 6-pounder, and its auxiliary splinter shield can be seen stowed on the side of the half-track.

An M4 of the 745th Tank Battalion provides overwatch as an M10 tank destroyer moves forward on 20 October during the final stage of the Aachen fighting. The German troops finally surrendered the next day when an M12 155mm gun motor carriage was used to reduce the commander's bunker at point-blank range.

A heavily camouflaged M10 3-inch gun motor carriage tank destroyer in action with Patton's Third Army in Lorraine.

Kampfgruppe Rink (Battle Group Rink) from SS Panzer Grenadier Regiment 1 attempted to evacuate its wounded out of Aachen on 20 October using their surviving Sd.Kfz. 251 half-tracks but were captured by an American tank roadblock on Oststrasse in Kohlscheid.

The 88mm flak gun was the most feared nemesis of American tanks during the 1944 fighting. This example has been abandoned by the road in Gradvillers and is seen on 13 October.

An M31 armored recovery vehicle provides assistance in repairing an M4 tank of the 66th Armored Regiment, 2nd Armored Division, in the city of Alsdorf, Germany, on 15 October. The crew appears to be replacing the T51 rubber block tracks seen on the left side with T49 metal grouser track. Once the wet autumn weather arrived in 1944, the smooth rubber block track developed a reputation as "suicide track" since it provided poor traction in the mud.

The crew of *Idle*, an M4 tank of the 3rd Battalion, 66th Armored Regiment, 2nd Armored Division, does its daily chores in the outskirts of Alsdorf on 15 October. While some of the crew handle suspension repair, one of them shaves.

An M31 (named *Invader*) of the 3rd Battalion, 66th Armored Regiment, 2nd Armored Division, pulls a damaged M4 across an engineer bridge near Palenberg, Germany, on 15 October.

The Wehrmacht made frequent use of captured equipment, especially French motor transport equipment. In 1943, some French Unic Kegresse P107 half-tracks were armored, and this particular example was captured by the Third Army. This Leichter Schützenpanzerwagen U304(f) differs from the more common style in that it is fully enclosed. This was done since this particular vehicle was used as a radio command vehicle for three tactical radios.

A heavily camouflaged M5A1 light tank (named *Malt*) from the 2nd Armored Division occupies a depression near Baeswiller on 19 October while a clutch of geese look on. The 2nd Armored Division, alongside the 30th Division, had pushed a gap through the Siegfried Line the previous week.

This photo provides a clear idea of how cramped the turret of the M8 75mm howitzer motor carriage was with the full crew in place. This is a vehicle from the 24th Cavalry Reconnaissance Squadron near Monshau, Germany, on 20 October.

An M7 105mm howitzer motor carriage of Battery B, 253rd Armored Field Artillery Battalion, sits under a camouflage net while awaiting firing instructions with Patton's Third Army in Lorraine on 23 October.

An M31 tank-recovery vehicle of the 32nd Armored Regiment, 3rd Armored Division, towing a disabled M3 half-track passes by an aqueduct near Stolberg, Germany, on 24 October. Although the new M32 tank-recovery vehicle was the authorized equipment in tank-maintenance units, a number of older battalions still employed the M31 through the end of the war.

Two German officers inspect an M5A1 of Company D, 747th Tank Battalion, knocked out in Geilenkirchen in late October while supporting the 29th Division. The officer on the right is pointing with his cane to the Culin hedgerow cutter, still fitted on the bow.

A view of the holding area of the 25th Ordnance Battalion near Eupen, Belgium, on 6 October. This shows one of the first shipments of the new M36 90mm gun motor carriage tank destroyers to the left. In the lower foreground is an M8 75mm howitzer motor carriage, and behind is an M4 105mm assault gun. Ordnance units were tasked with removing the waterproofing from armored vehicles that had recently arrived on board ships from the United States or Britain and preparing them to be issued to combat units.

The first M36 90mm gun motor carriages arrived in France in September, but they were not commonly deployed until October because of the need to train the crews and create adequate logistical support. Here, a unit trains on the new vehicles in France on 14 October.

This interesting comparison view shows the M10 3-inch gun motor carriage in front of one of the new M36 90mm gun motor carriages in Stolberg with the 703rd Tank Destroyer Battalion on 24 October. The new M36 helped redress the problem of dealing with heavier German tanks such as the Panther and Tiger I.

A close-up view inside the turret of a M36 90mm gun motor carriage near Toul, France, on 24 October. As is evident in this view, tank destroyer crews usually wore the normal steel helmet in combat, as the tanker's helmet offered no ballistic protection.

U.S. artillery units occasionally used captured German artillery until stocks of captured ammunition were exhausted. Here, ordnance troops in Rheims prepare a number of 88mm PaK 43 antitank guns prior to being issued to U.S. Army artillery units.

This is a view of one of the captured 88mm PaK 43 antitank guns seen after being emplaced by the 733rd Field Artillery Battalion on 25 October. Curiously enough, the battery used a captured and repainted Sd.Kfz. 251 Ausf. D half-track as the prime mover for the gun.

Mud was a major obstacle in tank operations along the Siegfried Line in October–November because of the unusually wet weather. Here, a pair of M31 tank-recovery vehicles try to extract an M4 tank of the 747th Tank Battalion that became bogged down during operations on 29 October.

The rainy autumn of 1944 created mobility problems for tanks due to the mud. To improve the traction of the Sherman and other American tanks, the U.S. Army began to fit the tank tracks with extended end connectors, also known as duck bills, which increased the track area and so lowered ground pressure. Here, the crew of an M4 of the 3rd Armored Division fastens extended end connectors to the track of their tank in the Stolberg area on 31 October.

M10 3-inch gun motor carriage of the 818th Tank Destroyer Battalion in a night bivouac during the fighting in Lorraine on 29 October while supporting the 5th Infantry Division.

A Patterson antiaircraft half-track conversion on an M2 half-track serving with the 460th Anti-Aircraft Artillery Automatic-Weapons Battalion (Mobile) in Germany on 2 November. This view shows the characteristic skate ring around the M2 fighting compartment, and spare .50-caliber barrels can be seen wedged in behind the skate ring. The Maxson turret is fitted with a mechanical ring sight instead of the usual optical sight.

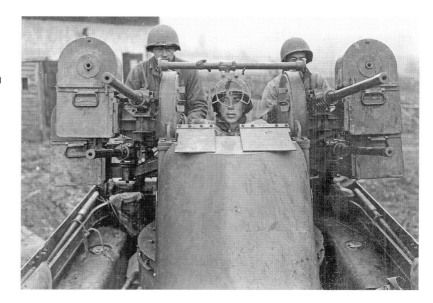

An M15A1 combination gun motor carriage of the 390th Anti-Aircraft Artillery Battalion in operation near Hoeville, France, on 3 November with Patton's Third Army. Although the Luftwaffe was very weak in the West, raids became more frequent in the autumn of 1944 as Allied forces pressed toward Germany.

The crew of an M3 half-track warm up around a stove near Zwiefall, Germany, on 3 November. Senior commanders often complained that armored infantry battalions equipped with half-tracks developed the appearance of "a gypsy caravan" because of their tendency to haul around anything that would fit in and on their half-tracks.

The intense fighting along the Siegfried Line and in Aachen convinced the U.S. Army of the need for a more heavily armored tank to provide close support. A solution was already in the works since February 1944 in the form of the M4A3E2 assault tank. This tank had the same 75mm gun as the normal M4, but had thicker armor on the turret and hull. This is an M4A3E2 in one of the ordnance yards in France on 4 November being prepared after shipment for issuance to a tank unit. It provides a good view of the new turret and the thick gun mantlet.

An M12 155mm gun motor carriage (named *Adolph's Assassin*) from Battery A, 991st Armored Field Artillery Battalion, prepares to fire near Kornelimünster, Germany, on 4 November. This view shows the 155mm gun elevated near its maximum. By this stage, the battalion's distinctive unit insignia has been painted over compared to photos of the unit seen earlier in this book.

An M10 3-inch gun motor carriage of the 893rd Tank Destroyer Battalion drives down a road toward Schmidt in the Hürtgen Forest in Germany on 4 November. The tank destroyers were brought up in an attempt to reinforce American infantry that had been subjected to a tank attack by Panthers of the 116th Panzer Division that day. Three M4 tanks were the first to arrive and blunted the German attack. The fighting in the Hürtgen Forest, mainly by U.S. Army infantry units, was one of the army's bloodiest campaigns in Europe in 1944–45.

The Hürtgen Forest fighting saw one of the rare uses of mobile rocket launchers by the U.S. Army with the deployment of the 18th Field Artillery Battalion for fire support. They were equipped with the 4.5-inch T32 Xylophone launcher, which consisted of two pairs of eight 7.5-foot launch tubes for a total of thirty-two tubes, mounted laterally on the rear of a 2.5-ton truck and firing the fin-stabilized M8 4.5-inch rocket. Here the crews are loading the launcher.

The crews of the 18th Field Artillery finish loading the Xylophone rocket launchers during operations on 26 November.

Here, the 18th Field Artillery Battalion fires a salvo of 4.5-inch rockets during the Hürtgen Forest fighting on 26 November.

The commander of an M5A1 light tank of F Troop, 113th Cavalry Recon Squadron, fires his .45-caliber Thompson submachine gun at targets near Kievelberg on 5 November.

The U.S. Army was still segregated in World War II, and this extended to tank units as well. Two black tank battalions saw combat service in Northwest Europe in 1944. The 761st Tank Battalion is the more famous, receiving the Presidential Unit Citation for its combat performance. This is an M4A3 (76mm) of the unit operating near Nancy, France, on 5 November.

The crewmen of Company D, 761st Tank Battalion, prepare their M5A1 light tanks.

An M4A3 (76mm) of Company A, 761st Tank Battalion, passes over a Bailey bridge in Vic-sur-Seille on 9 November during operations by Patton's Third Army in Lorraine.

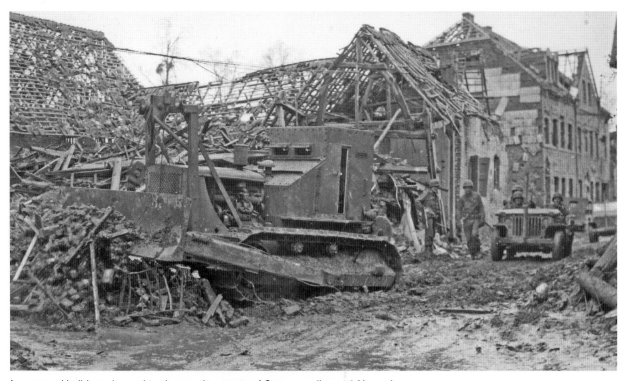

An armored bulldozer is used to clear up the streets of Gersonsweiler on 2 November.

Although few LVT amphibious tractors had been used in the Normandy campaign, they were deployed to the ETO in the autumn of 1944 for potential use in river crossings. Here is an LVT-4 entering the water on 7 November.

Another view of an LVT-4 during a training exercise on 7 November. These amtracs were often operated by tank battalions, and some practice was needed for crew familiarization.

Another problem addressed in the autumn of 1944 was the poor camouflage discipline of American tank crews. The First Army decided that the best solution would be for specialized engineer troops to take care of the matter. As a result, starting in October, the 602nd Engineer Camouflage Battalion developed a standardized method for applying camouflage paint to the tanks and adding a layer of Sommerfield matting over the main surfaces for the attachment of foliage. Entire tank battalions were painted during refits. The usual camouflage was black over olive drab, but some units had other colors added if paint was available. This is an M4A3 (76mm) of the 9th Armored Division, one of the units that was systematically camouflaged in the autumn of 1944.

This photo shows the 602nd Engineer Camouflage Battalion welding Sommerfield matting to the side of an M4A3 (76mm). Surprisingly, this tank still has sand shields fitted. There was an official policy in 12th Army Group to have sand shields removed as they interfered with maintenance.

This is a good example of an M4 (named *Bucks*) of the 4th Armored Division near Eupen, Germany, on 8 November after the Sommerfield matting has been added. They are listening to the results of the 1944 elections over the tank radio.

Surrendering German troops pass near an M4 tank of Company C, 735th Tank Battalion, near Vigny, France, during the fighting near Metz on 10 November.

An M16 antiaircraft half-track (named *Chief*) covering a river ford near Pont-a-Musson, France, on 10 November with the Third Army. The lack of internal stowage space due to the moving turret forced M16 crews to place most of their stowage over the bulkhead separating the driver's compartment and the fighting compartment or on the winch bumper frame.

An M10 3-inch gun motor carriage tank destroyer (named *Burnside*) in a dug-in position near Geilenkirchen in the U.S. Ninth Army's sector on 10 November. This town was on the border between Bradley's 12th Army Group and Montgomery's British 21st Army Group and was the scene of intense fighting through the late autumn of 1944.

A mud-covered M10 3-inch gun motor carriage of the 774th Tank Destroyer Battalion in support of the 5th Infantry Division around Metz on 12 November.

During mid-November, Patton's Third Army fought a series of engagements with the 11th Panzer Division in Lorraine, east of Chateau Salins. The 4th Armored Division engaged in a string of savage tank battles starting on 14 November near Guebling, which saw additional fighting on 19 November when the 761st Tank Battalion was supporting the 26th Infantry Division in the area. This is a scene along the road between Guebling and Bougaltrof showing three knocked-out Panther Ausf. G's and an Sd.Kfz. 250 of the 11th Panzer Division. In the foreground is an M4A3 (76mm) (named *All Hell*) of Company A, 35th Tank Battalion.

This is a view of the same scene from the opposite direction, showing three of the knocked-out Panthers from the 11th Panzer Division near Guebling.

Tank units frequently used the shelter of small towns when not committed to the fighting. These are M4A3 tanks of the 10th Armored Division on the streets of Tetange, Luxembourg, on 13 November.

An M10 3-inch gun motor carriage (named *Duke of Paduka*) of the 712th Tank Destroyer Battalion rolls through Metzervisse, Germany, on 17 November while in support of the 90th Division near the French Maginot Line fortifications. This unit had repulsed an armored attack by a battle group of the 25th Panzer Grenadier Division two days before near the Moselle River crossing, and on 14 November, it was part of a large U.S. armored force attempting to clear out the area on the east bank of the river north of the fortress city of Metz.

A view of the muddy fields around Conthil, France, on 14 November during fighting by CCB of the 4th Armored Division. This is the headquarters company of the 37th Tank Battalion, and the M4A3 (76mm) is *Thunderbolt VI*, the command tank of Lt. Col. Creighton Abrams, the battalion commander.

The 6th Armored Division received a number of M4A3E2 assault tanks in November, and this one was hit with six 88mm rounds during fighting near Neid, France, on 16 November. It is seen here being repaired by divisional maintenance crews.

Antitank ditches and other obstructions were a constant hindrance during operations along the Siegfried Line, leading to many improvisations by the armored engineers. One particularly popular innovation was the development of fittings that permitted M31 tank-recovery vehicles to carry and deploy treadway bridge sections to breach these gaps. This example is being used by the 17th Armored Engineer Battalion of the 2nd Armored Division near Beggendorf on 16 November at the start of Operation Queen, the failed offensive to reach the Roer River.

An M31 tank-recovery vehicle of the 2nd Armored Division near Loverich, Germany, on 18 November. Two large attachments have been welded to the final drive housings for use as an improvised treadway bridge layer.

The crew of an M4 medium tank refuel its tank in Beggendorf on 17 November.

German prisoners aid a wounded comrade past an M4 medium tank during the fighting on the German frontier, 18 November.

The gun of this M12 155mm gun motor carriage is in full recoil as it fires on a German pillbox near Grossenich, Germany, on 16 November. The substantial amount of gas created by firing kicked up a quite a storm of mud and dirt in front of the vehicle when fired at low elevation. These self-propelled guns were one of the most popular methods used by the First Army in its attempts to crack open bunkers along the Siegfried Line.

A patrol of infantry of the 29th Division passes a burned-out Panther of the 9th Panzer Division in Immendorf on November 16 at the start of Operation Queen.

The M20 armored utility vehicle was frequently used as a command car for senior commanders. This is the armored car of Gen. George S. Patton, commander of the Third Army, near Metz in November. Typical of command cars, it carries the red metal flag on the front with Patton's rank insignia. Sitting in the armored car with the general is Averill Harriman, American ambassador to the Soviet Union, who was visiting troops at the time.

An M4A1 of the 2nd Armored Division passes through Beggendorf on 17 November, one of the towns taken in the Aachen fighting that served as the First Army's salient toward the Roer River. The tank is carrying logs that were used to drop under the tanks as unditching beams if the tank got stuck in the mud. This was a common practice in the division during the November Roer River offensive.

Two M31 tank-recovery vehicles of the 2nd Armored Division during operations near Beggendorf on 17 November.

The crew of an M31 tank-recovery vehicle of the 6th Armored Division tries to extract its bogged vehicle during operations near Luppy, France, on 17 November.

Track repairs on an M7 105mm howitzer motor carriage of Battery C, 276th Armored Field Artillery Battalion, 6th Armored Division, near Brulange, France, on 17 November.

Daily chores, including swabbing out the barrel of the vehicle's 75mm howitzer are completed by the crew of an M8 75mm howitzer motor carriage.

An M7 105mm howitzer motor carriage of Battery A, 78th Armored Field Artillery Battalion, 2nd Armored Division, passes through Beggendorf, Germany, on 18 November during the fighting with the 9th Panzer Division.

Two M10s move up a steep forest road in the Hürtgen Forest on 18 November during attempts to reinforce American infantry units fighting in the forest during the second phase of the battle that started on 16 November. The U.S. units were not able to fight their way through the shell-shattered woods until early December, after suffering horrible casualties.

An M2A1 half-track car of the Third Army passes through the ruins of Xousse, France, in the Nancy area on 18 November. The side mine rack has been converted to carry jerricans of fuel or water.

On 19 November, an M3A1 half-track passes through a gap of metal antitank "dragon's teeth" that had been laid near the French-German border.

This Sd.Kfz. 251 Ausf. D half-track from Aufklärungs Abteilung 11 (11th Reconnaissance Battalion), 11th Panzer Division, was knocked out in the fighting for Grostenquin on 19 November by CCB, 6th Armored Division, during the fighting along the Maginot Line.

During the Roer River offensive in late November, the 84th Division was the northernmost American unit in Europe, rubbing shoulders with the British 43rd Infantry Division to its north. The town of Geilenkirchen straddled the British and American zones, so the British provided tank support for U.S. infantry operations in the town, as seen here on 19 November, with British Shermans providing fire support for the GIs.

Next to the Dutch border, Geilenkirchen was the start of a major line of German fortifications and mine fields. So British Crab flail tanks helped the U.S. 84th Division clear approaches near the town during the 19 November fighting.

While not as common a practice as in Italy, tanks in Northwest Europe were sometimes used to provide indirect artillery fire support. This M4A1 of the 32nd Armored Regiment, 3rd Armored Division, along with other tanks from the unit are being used as improvised artillery during the Roer River offensive on 19 November.

An enormous heap of 75mm ammunition transport containers have built up alongside an M4 medium tank being used to provide artillery fire support near Vicht, Germany, on 17 November.

An M4A1 dozer tank from Company I, 3rd Battalion, 66th Armored Regiment, 2nd Armored Division, clears a road during the Roer River offensive on 19 November. It ran over a mine on its right side, which has bent the M1 dozer assembly and ripped up the front bogie.

An M5A1 light tank (named *Bric*) from the 2nd Armored Division sits in a crater after having its front bogie blown off by a mine near Loverich, Germany, in late November. The fighting for the Roer area took place in very muddy conditions, which made it difficult to employ armor.

One of the first units into combat with the new M4A3E2 assault tank was the 743rd Tank Battalion, which was allotted fifteen in November while supporting the 30th Infantry Division. This tank was knocked out near Fronhoven in late November after having been hit by four 88mm rounds from an antitank gun about 800 yards away near Lohn. One bounced off the glacis plate and two off the mantlet before a lucky hit actually entered the telescope opening. Although not immediately apparent, this vehicle was fitted with a flamethrower in the hull machine-gun position. This shot provides a unique view of the contours of the lower turret.

This German StuG IV assault gun was abandoned in a shell hole after having suffered a catastrophic internal ammunition fire, which blew off its roof.

Another M4A3E2 assault tank of the 743rd Tank Battalion was knocked out in late November near Fronhoven after having run over an American mine, immobilizing it. It was then hit by eight 88mm antitank projectiles at a range of about 800 yards. One round penetrated the right sponson and set the tank on fire, but the other rounds failed to penetrate. The M4A3E2 was the only U.S. tank able to absorb this amount of punishment.

This is a front view of the same M4A3E2 knocked out near Fronhoven. An 88mm hit on the glacis plate obliterated some sand bags on the hull front. Three other hits are evident on the front, including one near the gun tube, one on the upper edge of the mantlet, and one on the upper edge of the glacis plate.

The turret interior of the Sherman was more spacious on the left side to permit the loader to access the gun. This is a view down into the loader's station of an M4A3 of the 774th Tank Battalion near Welfrang, Luxembourg, on 20 November. He is placing rounds in the forward wet stowage bin on the floor. The coaxial .30-caliber machine-gun breech can be seen immediately above his left shoulder, and the gun breech to the right of the photo.

An M8 75mm howitzer motor carriage of the 82nd Armored Reconnaissance Battalion, 2nd Armored Division, leads a column through Setterich, Germany, on 20 November during the fighting with the 9th Panzer Division. The open turret of the M8 75mm howitzer motor carriage left the crew exposed to the wet autumn weather, and a tarp was often draped over the opening to shield against the cold rain.

An M8 armored car of the 17th Cavalry Group, supporting the Ninth Army, passes the wreck of a German StuG III assault gun from the 3rd Panzer Grenadier Division in Kinzweiller, Germany, on 21 November. The town was taken on 19 November by the 117th Infantry Regiment, heavily supported by armor.

Pvt. Robert Starkey of the 16th Infantry, 1st Infantry Division, stands beside the burnt-out hulk of the Jagdpanzer IV tank destroyer he knocked out with his bazooka near Hamich, Germany, on 22 November. The bazooka explosion detonated the vehicle's ammunition, leading to a catastrophic internal fire that blew open the vehicle superstructure.

A Panther Ausf. G of II./Panzer Regiment 33, knocked out during the fighting around Immendorf and photographed on 23 November.

An M36 90mm gun motor carriage of Company C, 607th Tank Destroyer Battalion, takes up position in Metz on 20 November. Patton's Third Army made a failed attempt to seize the city in September and finally succeeded on 19 November when two infantry regiments and Task Force Bacon made their way into the city.

Another view of the same M36 taken a day later in Metz, with the French civilians finally emerging from their basements. Metz is a fortress city on the German-French frontier that has often been contested. Patton later boasted that his troops were the first to capture the fortress city since Attila the Hun in 415.

An M10 from a tank destroyer battalion of Patton's Third Army near Fort Koenigsmacker in the Metz defensive belt on 21 November. This unit was supporting the 90th Division and Task Force Bacon during the final assault on Metz, where resistance finally collapsed the next day after having held out for almost two months. This vehicle appears to have an armored roof fitted over the rear of the turret, but it is obscured by the tarp.

American troops advance through the outskirts of Metz as the German defenses were in the final stage of collapse after two months of determined resistance. Behind the GI is an M8 light armored car and an abandoned 88mm PaK 43 antitank gun.

The Flakpanzer IV Wirbelwind was a quadruple 20mm FlaK 38 mounted in an open turret on Pz.Kpfw. IV hulls. These were first deployed in France in the late summer of 1944, and this example was knocked out during the fighting around Metz.

This Jagdpanzer 38(t) Hetzer was knocked out by a bazooka hit during the fighting in the U.S. Ninth Army's sector near Aldenhoven on 21 November.

A Jagdpanzer IV from the 11th Panzer Division knocked out in the fighting with the 6th Armored Division near St. Jean Rohrbach on 22 November. The gun mantlet was knocked off by a tank-gun hit.

This Sd.Kfz. 250/9 was captured in France in 1944 from the 116th Panzer Division and is on the later Neu chassis with the Hangelafette gun mount.

A rear view of the Sd.Kfz. 250/9 of the 116th Panzer Division showing the division's standard leaping greyhound insignia, as well as the tactical insignia for a half-track reconnaissance unit. There is also a unit insignia in the shield to the right.

One of the main problems facing tank crews in the autumn of 1944 was the poor mobility of the M4 in muddy conditions. This new M4A3 (76mm) has completely bogged down in the mud while supporting the 84th Division during fighting in Germany on 24 November.

This rear view of the same M4A3 (76mm) tank shows that it is fitted with the T49 metal grouser tracks, one of the better solutions for muddy conditions compared to the rubber block track but still far from perfect.

One of the most serious tactical shortcomings in American tanks was the difficulty in communicating with neighboring infantry. The tank radios could not communicate with the infantry's radios. The solution was either to rack-mount an infantry radio like the SCR-300 into some tanks or to attach an exterior phone to the tank. This is an M4 of the 709th Tank Battalion with an exterior phone added inside a .30-caliber metal ammunition box. It is put to use here during operations with the 81st Division near Zweifall on 24 November.

In the autumn of 1944, two secret Leaflet tank battalions, the 738th and 739th, were converted into specialized tank battalions for the use of minefield-clearing equipment. These had a company with eighteen T1E1 mine rollers, two companies with twelve T1E3 mine-roller tanks, and six dozer tanks. The 739th Tank Battalion (Special) was deployed with the Ninth Army on 24 November. This M4 is fitted with the T1E3 mine rollers and is passing through Beggendorf, Germany, on 10 December.

An interesting photo of an E4-5 flamethrower mounted on an M4 tank of the 709th Tank Battalion near Zweifall, Germany, on 24 November. The photo is doubly interesting as the tank is still fitted with one of the rare "Green dozer" hedgerow cutters more commonly associated with the 747th Tank Battalion in Normandy.

An M12 155mm gun motor carriage (named *Buccaneer*) prepares for a fire mission in France on 25 November. The crew waits behind with another round, and the gunner at the far right can be seen holding another propellant bag charge.

An M4A3 (76mm) of the 6th Armored Division disabled by a German mine near Hellimer and Grostenquin on 25 November. It has become thoroughly trapped in the mud.

This shows the same tank a few days later. Engineers have marked the vehicle with tape to prevent the curious from stumbling into the minefield. The tank is so deeply bogged in the mud that an armored-recovery vehicle would be needed to repair it. In the days since it was knocked out, it has become draped with field telephone wires as well as a means to keep the wires out of the mud and puddles.

The M4's floatation problem in mud became even worse after the troops began adding improvised sand-bag armor on the hull front and hull sides. This is an M4A3 (76mm) of the 743rd Tank Battalion near Eschweiler, Germany, in November.

The solution to the floatation problem was to attach extenders to the track end connectors, and these can be seen on this tank from Company C, 69th Tank Battalion, 6th Armored Division. These were given various nicknames by the troops, such as "duck bills" or "duck feet."

This close-up shows the extended end connectors fitted to the track. The extra several inches of ground contact reduced the overall ground pressure of the tank, improving its mobility in muddy terrain.

Troops from the 531st Heavy Maintenance (Tanks) Company tighten the track tension on an M4A3 (105mm) at the maintenance yard in Etain, France, on 27 November. They have just added duck-bill extenders to the track.

The crew of a new M4A3 (105mm) assault gun shown in the previous photo try out the new duck-bill extenders in the yard at the Etain tank depot in November.

An M4 (105mm) assault gun of the 3rd Armored Division sits well concealed under improvised camouflage in the ruins of Eschweiler on 26 November during the Roer River offensive.

During fighting near Freialdenhoven on 28 November, this King Tiger heavy tank from schwere Panzer Abteilung 506 (506th Heavy Tank Battalion) was hit repeatedly by tank destroyers from the 702nd Tank Destroyer Battalion, 2nd Armored Division. The King Tiger was first stopped by a hit on the left track, and then an M36 90mm gun motor carriage hit the turret side from a range of 1,000 yards, destroying the tank. This King Tiger unit supported the 9th Panzer Division in a mid-November counter-attack to stop the 2nd Armored Division.

A good example of the M4A3E2 assault tank in service. This is an M4A3E2 of the 743rd Tank Battalion, supporting the 30th Infantry Division near Altdorf on 27 November. It has been reinforced with additional sand-bag armor on the glacis plate, which was then covered with camouflage netting.

An M12 155mm gun motor carriage of the 981st Field Artillery Battalion provides fire support for U.S. infantry formations during the bloody battles for the Hürtgen Forest near Kleinhau, Germany, on 30 November.

As in the case of the 2nd Armored Division, the 771st Tank Battalion had suffered from enough experiences of bogged-down tanks that its tanks carried unditching logs during the Roer fighting. Here, the headquarters company of the 771st Tank Battalion takes a breather in Welz on 29 November while supporting the 102nd Division's attempts to gain a foothold on the Roer River. The tanks are M4 assault guns, armed with a 105mm howitzer and used for indirect fire support of the battalion.

An M4 of the 6th Armored Division takes a break near a pock-marked pillbox of the Siegfried Line near Kappel, Germany, on 1 December.

An M18 76mm gun motor carriage tank destroyer crosses a length of treadway bridging. Besides being used to cross rivers, treadway bridge sections were also used by engineer units to cross antitank ditches or other terrain obstructions.

An M5A1 light tank of the 8th Tank Battalion, 4th Armored Division, helps to evacuate a wounded tanker in the muddy conditions on the Saar front on 1 December.

In early December, a number of amtracs were delivered to the divisional trains of the 6th Armored Division to familiarize crews in anticipation of river-crossing operations over the Roer and Rhine. This is an LVT-4 from the original batch delivered to Valette, France, on 2 December.

A pair of LVT-4 amtracs are given an inspection by crews from the 6th Armored Division prior to trials in local waterways. In the event, the 6th Armored Division did not use the LVTs in combat, though they were used on a limited scale by divisional engineer troops.

An LVT-4 in the hands of the 6th Armored Division during trials in marshy lands near Valette in early December. In early March 1945, the 747th Tank Battalion turned in its tanks and swapped them for seventeen LVT-2 and eight LVT-4s, which were used on 24–26 March for the Rhine crossing.

An LVT-4 returns from a test-spin in a local lake on 7 December with mud caked up on the tracks. As can be seen, this particular amtrac has several armor panels added over the pontoons to protect the crew and drive train.

A more commonly encountered tank destroyer in the winter of 1944–45 was the Sd.Kfz. 251/22, which mounted the 75mm PaK 40 on the standard army half-track. This particular vehicle belonged to the 11th Panzer Division, which was committed to the Saar fighting in December.

The final version of the German Sd.Kfz. 251/17 half-track had its 20mm autocannon in a small turret mount sometimes called the *Schwebelafette*. This particular example was captured in the Saar by Patton's Third Army.

During the last two weeks of November, the U.S. First and Ninth Armies conducted Operation Queen to push past Aachen to the Roer River. The area was tenaciously defended and included panzer units such as the 9th Panzer Division. This is a Panther Ausf. G captured during the fighting and being hauled away from the battlefield through Geilenkirchen by an M26 tractor on 4 December after the offensive. This M26 belonged to the 464th Ordnance Evacuation Company, U.S. Ninth Army.

A closer view of the M26 tractor towing the Panther through Geilenkirchen.

A rear view of the M26 tractor providing a clearer look at the Panther Ausf. G. The tracks have been removed from the tank to make it easier to haul on the road.

Because of shortages of flamethrower tanks, British tanks were often seconded to American units for support. In this case, a Churchill Crocodile of the 9020 Tank Squadron, 1st Fife and Forfar Yeomanry, was attached to the U.S. 2nd Armored Division during operations in late November along the Siegfried Line. Here, a Crocodile is attacking a target near Merkstein, Germany, on 3 December.

An M4A3E2 assault tank of the 745th Tank Battalion wades through the water and mud under a destroyed railroad viaduct in early December during the fighting for the industrial town of Langerwehe by the 1st Infantry Division.

The Sd.Kfz. 7/1 antiaircraft half-track mounted the quadruple 20mm FlaK 38. This particular example shows the armored cab configuration. It was captured by Patton's Third Army.

The Sd.Kfz. 7/2 antiaircraft half-track mounted the 37mm FlaK 36, and the markings appear to indicate a vehicle of the 3rd Company of Panzerjäger Abteilung 256 (256th Tank Destroyer Battalion). This example was captured by the Third Army in the Saar.

A close-up view of the front armored cab of an Sd.Kfz. 7/2.

An M4 of the 709th Tank Battalion uses the shelter of a shattered house on Kirchstrasse in the devastated town of Hürtgen on 5 December after the town was taken by the 121st Infantry. The M4 is still fitted with a "rhino" hedgerow cutter. In the foreground is a burned-out M4 tank lost in the earlier fighting on 28 November.

American troops inspect a knocked-out Sd.Kfz. 7/1 with a prominent hole through the front armor panel.

A GI inspects an Sd.Kfz. 251 Ausf. D found in a garage in Ederen during clean-up operations along the Roer River on 5 December. The half-track carries the name *Hannelore* and a tactical marking on the bow that is apparently that of the 9th Panzer Division, which defended the area until late November when it was pulled out to refit prior to the Ardennes offensive.

A group of M8 75mm howitzer motor carriages provides fire support for the 47th Armored Infantry Battalion, 5th Armored Division, during the fighting for the Hürtgen Forest on 7 December. By then, U.S. forces had finally fought their way to the eastern edge of the woods and on to the approaches to the Roer.

THE SIEGFRIED LINE   363

The ground is littered with spent 105mm howitzer casings near an M4 (105mm) assault gun of the HQ company, 70th Tank Battalion, providing fire support during the fighting near Schevenhütte, Germany, on 7 December.

The crew of an M4 tank of the 2nd Armored Division attach "duck bills" to their tank track during a refit in Baesweiller, Germany, on 5 December. The end connectors without "duck bills" can be seen in the left foreground; the end connectors with "duck bills" are seen on the track to the right.

An M7 105mm howitzer motor carriage (named *All American*) from Battery A, 231st Armored Field Artillery Battalion, 6th Armored Division, has been positioned on an improvised ramp to get higher elevation during a fire mission near Kleinbittersdorf, Germany, on 7 December. The logs on the side were a common sight in the autumn of 1944 and were used to help extract vehicles from the thick mud.

This Pz.Kpfw. 38(t) was knocked out by an M18 Hellcat of the 704th Tank Destroyer Battalion during the fighting along the Siegfried Line in the Saar near Ober Pearl in December. This obsolete tank was no longer in frontline service and was probably attached to a training company.

An M4 medium tank of the 2nd Armored Division advances through Dochamps, Belgium, on its way toward the fighting around Samree on 8 December. The snowfall at this time of the year was intermittent, with frequent cold rains washing away the snow.

An M4 tank fitted with a T1E3 Aunt Jemima mine roller moves down a road along the German border while supporting the 712th Tank Battalion and 30th Infantry Division on 10 December. The 739th Tank Battalion was one of two battalions specifically configured for mine-clearing operations and had one company with eighteen T1E1 mine rollers, two companies with twelve, and six dozer tanks.

A crew from the 739th Tank Battalion (SMX) mounts a T1E1 Earthworm mine exploder on the front of an M32B1 while supporting the 30th Division in Germany on 10 December.

A T1E3 Aunt Jemima of the 739th Tank Battalion (SMX) in operation near Beggendorf, Germany, on 10 December.

An M32 pushing a T1E1 Earthworm mine exploder of the 738th Tank Battalion (SMX) supports the 3rd Armored Division near Langerwehe, Germany, on 10 December.

Another view of the same tank with mine exploder prepares to clear a road near Beggendorf on 11 December. The M4 tank is fitted with nonstandard grouser stowage on the hull side.

One of the concerns about using the T1E3 was the effect of its combined fifty-four-ton weight when moved over treadway bridges. Here, the 739th Tank Battalion (SMX) tests an M4A1 pushing a T1E3 mine exploder on 10 December.

Another view of the test of a T1E3 mine exploder in Germany showing details of its configuration between the two roller assemblies.

The Roer front in November was a sea of mud, leading to many improvisations. Here, troops from the 39th Infantry, 9th Division, help the crew of an M4 tank of the 746th Tank Battalion attach a section of corduroy matting on the front of the tank on 10 December. That day, the division started a new attack on Merode along the Siegfried Line along with the 3rd Armored Division. The matting consisted of several logs tied together with wire and could be laid down as a carpet in front of the tank when particularly deep mud was encountered.

This German half-track ambulance was captured by the 121st Infantry, 8th Infantry Division, in the concluding phases of the Hürtgen fighting and is seen here on 6 December.

On 11 December, following the Hürtgen fighting, some GIs from the 3rd Armored Division look at a heavily camouflaged StuG III Ausf. G knocked out in the fighting around Obergeich the day before in an encounter with the 33rd Armored Regiment.

An M10 3-inch gun motor carriage tank destroyer advances through Hürtgen on 12 December while advancing toward the Roer battlefront.

On 11 December, the 2nd Battalion, 60th Infantry, 9th Division, teamed with Task Force Hogan of the 3rd Armored Division to assault the village of Geich beyond the Langerwehe industrial area. This is an evocative picture of the harsh field conditions during the winter of 1944 in Germany as two GIs huddle under the shelter of an M4 tank on 11 December. This tank has been fitted with an external tank telephone as can be seen in the form of the .30-caliber ammo box attached to the engine door above the head of the GI to the right.

An M18 76mm gun motor carriage in Immendorf, Germany, on 11 December. This view clearly shows the mud guards designed for this vehicle. These were frequently lost in action or removed by the crew as they interfered with maintenance on the suspension. Three weeks earlier, Immendorf had been the site of a major tank battle with the 9th Panzer Division.

A GI peers inside an M4 that has slid into a water-filled hole in the ruins of Düren, Germany, during the fighting there in December.

An M31 armored-recovery vehicle of the 463rd Ordnance Battalion tows an M4 tank of the 746th Tank Battalion that has struck a mine. The mine has completely blown off the lead bogie assembly. The M31 appears to be impressively armed, but in fact, the 75mm hull gun and 37mm turret gun are dummies intended to make it appear like the normal M3 medium tank on which it was based.

A late-production M10 3-inch gun motor carriage of the 773rd Tank Destroyer Battalion, Third Army, crosses the Saar over a treadway bridge on 12 December. While much of the Third Army was fighting around Bastogne, the XX Corps remained in the Saar River area in preparation for a later offensive into Germany. This particular M10 has a metal cover over the turret rear and pipes welded to the four corners of the hull to attach stakes for camouflage.

An ordnance collection yard in Verdun accumulates worn-out and battle-damaged equipment in Patton's Third Army sector. In the foreground are a pair of M4 medium tanks while behind the tank on the left is a captured German Jagdpanzer IV tank destroyer.

A 57mm antitank gun crew manhandles its weapon on the streets of a town in the Saar on 12 December during the fighting there by the Third Army. This view illustrates why the infantry was reluctant to acquire heavier antitank guns as the 57mm gun was at the outer limit of the size and weight that could be managed by a crew.

The crew of an M4 tank of the 709th Tank Battalion watch as a column of German prisoners walk by in Lammersdorf on 14 December. The fighting for this stretch of the Siegfried Line by the 78th Division continued over the next few days and even after the start of the Battle of the Bulge a few miles south in the Monschau Forest two days later.

Shortages of equipment occasionally led to substitution. This M4A3 (76mm) is being used by the 629th Tank Destroyer Battalion in Gurzenich, Germany, during the fighting there on 14 December. The battalion was normally equipped with the M10 3-inch gun motor carriage.

A wrecker truck is used to recover an M32B1 of the 771st Tank Battalion. It has lost a track near Immendorf on 14 December.

A pair of Jagdpanzer 38 assault guns of Panzerjäger Abteilung 272 (272nd Tank Destroyer Battalion) were disabled along Hauptstrasse in Kesternich during the bitter fighting in December between the 272nd Volksgrenadier Division and the U.S. 78th Division in the days before the outbreak of the Ardennes offensive.

British Crocodile flamethrower tanks provide support for the U.S. 2nd Armored Division during the fighting around Alsdorf. An M4A1(76mm) can be seen in the foreground and two British Churchill Crocodiles in the distance.

In anticipation of the Ardennes fighting, German panzer units were brought up to near full strength. The schwere Panzer Abteilung 506 (506th Heavy Tank Battalion) was rebuilt, but lost this tank (tactical number 2-11) near Geronsweiller on 15 December, a day before the start of the Ardennes offensive. It was recovered by the U.S. 129th Ordnance Battalion.

This King Tiger of schwere Panzer Abteilung 506 is driven away by a U.S. Army ordnance team near Gersonsweiler on 15 December.

Under new ownership. The Geronswiler King Tiger has been given new markings so that it can be safely driven back through American lines.

Many American tank battalions were not keen to burden their tanks with T34 Calliope launchers, so the 350th Ordnance Battalion, attached to the 7th Armored Group, tried mounting one of the launchers on a captured German Sd.Kfz. 251 Ausf. D half-track as seen here on 15 December.

The Calliope rocket launcher required extensive modification to the Sd.Kfz. 251, including a large cut on the right side armor to accommodate the elevating arm.

Another view of the Sd.Kfz. 251 half-track converted by the 350th Ordnance Battalion to carry a 4.5-inch Calliope multiple rocket launcher.

This shows the improvised Sd.Kfz. 251 Calliope launcher being fired in Belgium on 15 December.

An M7 105mm howitzer motor carriage moves through Hagenau during the fighting along the German border on 15 December in the days before the Ardennes offensive.

An M10 3-inch gun motor carriage of the 654th Tank Destroyer Battalion covers a street intersection while supporting the 134th Infantry, 35th Division, during fighting in Habkirchen, Germany, on 15 December.

Even though the Battle of the Bulge had already started in neighboring Belgium, the fighting continued along the Siegfried Line to push out of the dreaded Hürtgen Forest. Here, an M4A3 (76mm) from the 774th Tank Battalion and an M10 tank destroyer move past a StuG III Ausf. G in Gurzenich in support of the 83rd Division on 17 December. By this stage, the U.S. First Army had emerged from the Hürtgen Forest and reached its objective on the plains approaching the Roer River.

Another view of an M4 tank supporting the 83rd Division while clearing out Gurzenich on 17 December. This may be an M4A3E2 assault tank, although precise identification of the type is made difficult by the camouflage on the turret. The commander's cupola has a .30-caliber light machine gun mounted.

One of the 57mm antitank gun platoons in the 104th Division decided it would rather operate this captured German StuG III assault gun than its little 57mm gun. The vehicle is seen passing through Imden on 17 December with its new owners.

An M8 light armored car of the 86th Cavalry Reconnaissance Squadron (Mechanized), 6th Armored Division, passes through a German street barrier on the outskirts of St. Nikolaus on 17 December.

An M32B1 tank-recovery vehicle tries to help extricate a T1E3 mine roller of the 739th Tank Battalion that has become bogged down while conducting mine-clearance operations for the 30th Infantry Division on 19 December. The weight of these mine rollers was one of their main drawbacks, especially in the muddy weather typical during the autumn of 1944 along the German frontier.

When one M32B1 did not prove enough to move the disabled M4 and T1E3 mine-roller combination, another M32 was brought in to assist. It has been fitted with sand bags for added protection. Notice also that the M4 tank has a section of corduroy matting on the hull side.

A close-up of an M45 Maxson turret of the 473rd Anti-Aircraft Artillery Automatic-Weapons Battalion (Self-Propelled) on Christmas Day in Ubach, Germany.

Tank destroyers were not organic to armored divisions, but most armored divisions had at least one tank destroyer battalion attached during most of the fighting in the ETO. This is one of the new M36 90mm gun motor carriages of the 703rd Tank Destroyer Battalion supporting the 3rd Armored Division near Malempre, Belgium, on 16 December.

Here, a British Crab flail tank detonates a mine near Geilenkirchen while supporting the U.S. XII Corps on Christmas Day.

CHAPTER 10

Across the Vosges to the Rhine

THE MOST SUCCESSFUL ALLIED campaign of the autumn is also the least celebrated. The 6th Army Group was given the task of pushing to the Rhine in Alsace. There were two approaches to the Rhine plains, either over the Vosges Mountains or through the heavily fortified Belfort Gap. The U.S. Seventh Army was assigned to assault over the Vosges and through their mountain passes, while the French First Army attacked the Belfort Gap.

After frustrations through much of October, the main Allied attacks kicked off on 13 November. The French First Army used its two armored divisions and its experienced colonial infantry divisions to liberate Belfort and Mulhouse. The French reached the Rhine on 19 November. Meanwhile, the Seventh Army had several divisions that had developed sound mountain-fighting experience in the Italian campaign and managed to push through the Vosges via two mountain passes. Although armor was used in a supporting role in the fighting, this was primarily an infantry contest.

The Seventh Army's armored reserve at this point was the French 2e DB, which remained under American command through most of 1944 because of political differences between Leclerc and the French First Army leaders. When the Seventh exited the mountain passes to the Rhine plains, the 2e DB was unleashed and made a dash for the provincial capital of Strasbourg, which was liberated on 25 November. Gen. Jacob Devers, the 6th Army Group's commander, proposed to leap-frog the Rhine and advance up its eastern bank in order to unhinge German defenses standing in Patton's way, but Eisenhower was skeptical of this approach. Instead, the Seventh Army was given the task of striking toward Hagenau and the Wissembourg gap in the hopes of undermining German defenses on the western bank of the Rhine, while the French First Army continued to struggle against a large pocket of German troops still holding out on the western side of the Rhine around Colmar.

A U.S. Seventh Army M7 105mm howitzer motor carriage crosses a hastily repaired bridge near Remiremont on 24 September. Typical of vehicles that had served in Italy, it is a 1942-production vehicle upgraded in the field with a piece of armor welded behind the machine-gun pulpit to extend the side panel upward to cover the hull ammunition racks. It is also refitted with the later suspension bogies.

A French M4A4 of the 2e Cuirassiers, 1e DB (French 1st Armored Division) knocked out during the fighting on the approaches to Alsace in the autumn of 1944.

On 21 September, American troops inspect a 37mm Flakpanzer, popularly dubbed the *Möbelwagen* ("furniture truck"), abandoned in Vertigny during the German retreat into the Vosges Mountains. This was a specialized antiaircraft version of the Pz.Kpfw. IV tank armed with a 37mm automatic cannon.

September 1944 was one of the wettest on record in Europe, with many fields being turned to mud by the rain. Here, an M4 of the 59th Armored Field Artillery Battalion's HQ company is retrieved by a wrecker after having become bogged down in a field near Plombieres on 26 September.

In the autumn of 1944, the Germans began deploying surplus tank guns on expedient pedestal mounts to create hasty defensive lines along the German frontier. One of the first of these guns in action was an SK-L IIa pedestal 88mm KwK 43 gun from Festungs-PaK-Verband XXVI (XXVI Fortress Anti-Tank Unit) on a standard Betonfundament concrete pad positioned in the Saverne gap in the High Vosges to block access to Phalsbourg as part of the Vosges Line. This particular gun was originally intended for the Jagdpanther tank destroyer. This position fell during the fighting with the U.S. Seventh Army in November, one of thirty-two of these guns lost in this campaign.

This Panther turret was intended for emplacement as a fixed *Panzerturm* in the Saales Pass in November on a concrete bunker, but it was overrun before completion. This is an example of a *Pantherturm-Stellung* based on a surplus tank turret rather than a new-production *Ostwallturm*, which was a dedicated fortification Panther turret with thicker roof armor.

An M4A1 of the 756th Tank Battalion knocked out during the fighting in Vagney, France, on 8 October. This is a tank from the early-production batch of about 250 M4A1s with the direct vision ports for the driver. Like many veterans of the Italian campaign, the 756th Tank Battalion had a large number of old tanks when it arrived in southern France.

The men of an M4 (105mm) assault gun crew of the HQ Company, 191st Tank Battalion, cook food during a lull in the fighting near Rambervillers, France, on 15 October. The M4 (105mm) was fitted with a 105mm howitzer instead of the normal 75mm gun and was used to provide indirect fire support for the battalion. In 1944, most tank battalions had six of these attached to their headquarters company.

An M4A3 (76mm) medium tank of the 756th Tank Battalion, supporting the 3rd Infantry Division near Brouvelieures, France, in October. The crew has started to weld metal strips to the glacis plate as the first step in applying a layer of sand bags to add further protection to the tank. The M4 was not well protected against typical German antitank weapons like the Panzerfaust and Panzerschreck, which led to many improvised armor improvements in the field.

Riflemen of the Japanese-American 442nd Infantry Regiment near Bruyeres pass by a disabled German Leichte SPW U304(f), an armored conversion of the captured French Unic Kegresse P107 half-track.

The Polish TKS tankette was used for antipartisan patrols by German forces on the Russian front and in the Balkans and was rarely encountered in the West.

During the campaign along the Meurthe River, the 21st Panzer Division was committed against the U.S. Seventh Army in October. This is a pair of Panthers of the division knocked out near Autrey to the east of Vesoul in a tank battle with American forces in late October.

The M4 (105mm) assault gun was a prodigious consumer of ammunition since it was normally used on fire-support missions like normal field artillery. Here, one of the crewman helps load a 105mm round through the shell ejection port on the left turret side. The stenciled 5698GG marking is a shipping code for the unit.

Two M31's of the 753rd Tank Battalion recover an overturned truck near Les Rouges Eaux, France, on 22 October. The M31 nearest the camera is named *Sad Sack*.

A close-up view of the M31 *Sad Sack* during the recovery effort by the 753rd Tank Battalion on 22 October.

An M4A1 of the Seventh Army knocked out near La Salle, France, on 3 November. The GI points to where a German antitank shell penetrated the hull armor and then passed through the turret race. This is an early-production M4A1 with the early-pattern bogie assemblies. The Seventh included many units that had fought in 1943 in the Italian theater and so had a large amount of older equipment.

An M4 medium tank and M8 armored car of the 753rd Tank Battalion pass by the town church of Brouvelierures while supporting the 36th Division during the fighting for the Vosges mountain passes on 29 October.

The rainy conditions in the autumn of 1944 are graphically shown in this view of an M4A3 (105mm) assault gun of the 756th Tank Battalion, seen near Les Rouges Eaux on 8 November.

A 75mm PaK 40 auf Chenillette (f) abandoned in Vesoul. This was a Becker conversion done in France to reinforce the poorly equipped garrison forces in 1942–43. This type of conversion was more commonly seen with the 21st Panzer Division in Normandy than in Alsace, but some elements of the division served in the Lorraine campaign in the autumn.

An M12 155mm gun motor carriage of Battery C, 557th Field Artillery Battalion, near Morteau, France, on 15 November. This photo shows the recoil chocks placed under the front tracks and the hoops for the camouflage net erected over the gun compartment. This vehicle is unusual in that it is still fitted with the front portion of the sand skirts, a feature not commonly seen on the M12 155mm gun motor carriage in Europe.

A rare example of a late-production Sd.Kfz. 251/17 half-track armed with 2-centimeter KwK 38 is seen knocked out in the ruins of La Bourgance during the fighting with the 3rd Infantry Division on 15 November in the Vosges Mountains.

An M4 tank is covered in a fresh coat of wet snow on a roadside near Belmont, France, after having run over a mine on 12 November. The tank has already been roped off by engineers with white cloth tape, the usual precaution in mined areas.

An M2A1 command post vehicle of the 56th Armored Infantry Battalion, 12th Armored Division, lands in France at Le Havre from an LST on 15 November. This was the second American armored division assigned to the Seventh Army and the last to arrive. The French 2e DB and U.S. 14th Armored Division were already in combat in Alsace by this time.

The 1e Spahis, the reconnaissance element of the French 2e DB, pass through Brouville on 17 November during the approach to the Alsatian capitol of Strasbourg. The unit was equipped with the M5A1 light tank and M8 light armored car.

An M10 3-inch gun motor carriage tank destroyer takes up covered positions in the Vosges foothills during the fighting around St. Benoit in November.

On 17 November, the crewmen of an M4A3 (76mm) tank of the 712th Tank Battalion perform a "show and tell" for a Signal Corps photographer to demonstrate how a German Panzerschreck rocket launcher knocked out their tank near Metzervisse. The crewman on the right is showing the small penetration hole caused by the rocket's shaped-charge warhead.

A German Sd.Kfz. 251/21 with triple machine-gun mount, possibly from Panzer Brigade 106, was knocked out by Seventh Army artillery in St. Michel-sur-Meurthe during the fighting on 20 November.

The effect of a Panzerfaust antitank rocket could be catastrophic if it detonated the internal ammunition of an M4. This M4A2 of the French 5e DB, serving with the U.S. 6th Army Group in Alsace, had its turret blown off after a Panzerfaust set off its ammunition during the fighting in Issans on 18 November. The tank's hull can be seen in the distance.

An M10 3-inch gun motor carriage with the XV Corps during the fighting on the approaches to Sarrebourg in late November. This is probably one of the M10's of the RBFM, the tank destroyer battalion of the French 2e DB, which was the main armored element of the attack.

Infantry of the French 3rd Moroccan Infantry Division (3e DIM), supported by camouflaged Sherman tanks, pass through Rochesson during the fighting along the Rhine in November.

An M4A2 tank of the French 5e DB with infantry support moves into the outskirts Belfort on 20 November during the efforts to penetrate the Belfort Gap onto the Alsatian plains along the Rhine. Although the Free French Army was equipped mainly with American equipment and uniforms, some French armored units managed to locate prewar French crew helmets, as can be seen on several of the troopers behind the tank.

An M4A2 tank of the French 5e DB crosses a treadway bridge near Belfort on 20 November during the siege of that city. Logs were carried on the tanks in corduroy bundles that were placed under the track in muddy ground conditions to improve traction.

Fontenay, an M4A4 of the 2e Cuirassiers, French 1e DB, takes part in the attack on the Gestapo headquarters in Mulhouse on 22 November.

A pair of M4A4 medium tanks of the 2e Cuirassiers, 1e DB, during the fighting for Mulhouse on 22 November. One of the key cities in the Belfort gap, Mulhouse covered access to the Rhine plains and so was a key objective of the 6th Army Group's offensive.

Two French M4A2 tanks of the French 1e DB fire on German defenders near the Lefevre Kaserne in Mulhouse on 23 November during the attack of the French First Army beyond Belfort. Obscured by the smoke is an M7 105mm howitzer motor carriage in the background in front of the two tanks.

On 23 November, the Panzer Lehr Division began a counterattack from Sarre-Union against the Seventh Army, hitting two regiments of the 44th Division. This Panther Ausf. G was knocked out near Schalbach on 25 November during fighting with the 114th Infantry. There is a bazooka hit evident on the hull side immediately below the turret. The Panzer Lehr was forced to abandon the attack when the 4th Armored Division launched a flank attack from Fenetrange with its Combat Command B.

M4A1 medium tanks refuel and rearm in the town square of Sarrebourg on 24 November. The nearest tank carries the name *Audrey*.

GIs look over a well-camouflaged 88mm PaK 43 antitank gun positioned in front of Hotel Mazeran in the Saales Pass on 25 November during the fighting in the Vosges Mountains.

The 14th Armored Division was one of the last American armored divisions to arrive in France, docking at Marseilles on 31 October. It was committed to the fighting in the Vosges region on 20 November, and here, some M4A3 tanks of its Combat Command A move forward near Cirey on 23 November.

After the Seventh Army burst out of the Vosges in mid-November, Gen. Alexander Patch unleashed his mobile exploitation force, the French 2e Division Blindée. The advance of Leclerc's 2e DB was so sudden and unexpected that when the French tanks burst into Strasbourg on 23 November, the citizens were going about their business with no expectation of the drama that was unfolding. This photo was taken a few days after the liberation, with the damaged Notre Dame cathedral in the background.

An M10 of the RBFM, French 2e DB, on the approaches to Strasbourg during the mid-November fighting.

An M10 3-inch gun motor carriage of the RBFM, knocked out in Strasbourg on 25 November.

The M4 (named *Brive-la-Gaillarde*) of Lieutenant Krebs, leader of the 3rd Platoon, 3rd Squadron, 12th Cuirassiers, French 2e Division Blindée, advances through Strasbourg on 25 November. It carries the distinctive Cross of Lorraine insignia unique to this division, which always fought in American armies, in this case with Patch's Seventh Army. The other French armored divisions of the French First Army carried the 1804 Napoleonic flag instead.

The rainy conditions in the autumn of 1944 undermined roads and led to accidents like this one where a M4A3 (76mm) of Company A, 781st Tank Battalion, slid off the road in Lamberg after the bank collapsed under its weight. It is being recovered by one of the new M32 armored-recovery vehicles.

A GI inspects a StuG III in Molsheim during the fighting in the Alsace region of France. Two of its side skirts have been removed and placed in front to provide improvised camouflage.

A GI looks over an M4 tank of the 756th Tank Battalion knocked out by a German StuG III during an engagement near Mutzig on 26 November while supporting Task Force Whirlwind from the 3rd Division.

GIs from Company B, 114th Infantry, 44th Division, hop aboard M5A1 light tanks of the 749th Tank Battalion in Struth, France, on 28 November following the fall of Sarrebourg. By this stage, the sand bags added to the glacis plate have become a heap of mud from the wet weather.

M4A3's of the 14th Armored Division pass by three other Shermans knocked out by German mines near Barr, France, on 29 November. These are very late-production M4A3 tanks, evident from the late-style 75mm gun turret with its improved commander's vision cupola and the raised rear bustle casting.

An M3A1 half-track (named *Baby Bastard No. 1*) passes the burning wreck of an M4A3 (76mm) medium tank of the 48th Tank Battalion, 14th Armored Division, knocked out during the fighting in Barre on 29 November.

A column of M4A3 tanks from Combat Command A, 14th Armored Division, halts in the Alsatian village of Scherwiller on 2 December during the Seventh Army's assault toward Selestat. These are late-production vehicles with the oval loader's hatch and the commander's all-round vision cupola.

The crew of an M18 76mm gun motor carriage of the 602nd Tank Destroyer Battalion loads ammunition in Saar-Union on 2 December. The ammunition came packed in black fiber-board containers, and the crew can be seen removing them from the tubes to load in the ammunition racks inside the M18.

Panzer support for the German Nineteenth Army in the Belfort Gap was scant. The badly depleted Panzer Brigade 106 served as its fire brigade, rushing from spot to spot in hopes of averting catastrophe. One of its Pz.Kpfw. IV tanks is seen on fire after being hit by bazooka fire during a skirmish with the French 4e DMM in the Hardt Woods near Pont-du-Bouc, north of Mulhouse, during the fighting for the Belfort gap in the first days of December.

Riflemen of the 313rd Infantry, 79th Division, advance into Bischwiller on 8 December while supported by M5A1 light tanks of Company D, 191st Tank Battalion.

An M7 105mm howitzer motor carriage of the 143rd Cannon Company, 36th Division, conducts a fire mission on the outskirts of Ribeauville, France, on 9 December with the ground nearby littered with propellant casings and fiberboard shipping tubes.

An M4A3 (76mm) of the 191st Tank Battalion passes by the wrecked "Gasthaus zu Fussball" ("Football Hotel") along the Strasbourg-Hagenau road on 9 December while supporting the 79th Infantry Division.

An M4A3 (76mm) tank of the 191st Tank Battalion supports infantry of the 79th Division during the fighting for the town of Hagenau north of Strasbourg on 10 December, part of a broader VI Corps offensive in Alsace.

An M2A1 half-track of the 495th Field Artillery Battalion, 12th Armored Division, disabled by a mine in Bining, France, on 10 December. Once again, a stowage bin has been fitted to the rear.

Some of the dozer tanks operated by the Seventh Army had been converted in British REME (Royal Electrical and Mechanical Engineers) workshops in Italy and were based on M4A4 tanks, like this one from the 63rd Engineers, knocked out by a mine near Enchenberg, France, on 10 December. The M4A4 version of the Sherman was seldom used by the U.S. Army in Europe; most were earmarked for Lend-Lease supply to Britain.

An M5A1 of the 12th Armored Division lies disabled in the streets of Bining on 10 December after an artillery strike near its weakly protected rear area damaged the engine.

This M2A1 is being used as the command post—with its battalion insignia on the side—for the 56th Armored Infantry Battalion, 12th Armored Division, in France in December 1944. These command-post vehicles usually had the interior covered by a regulation tarp to protect the radio equipment, especially in foul winter weather. The similarity of the stowage bin on this half-track suggests that the divisional ordnance unit may have constructed standardized designs.

During the Alsace fighting in December, an ordnance unit in the Seventh Army built a 4.5-inch rocket launcher on a jeep using M14 launch tubes designed for fitting on aircraft.

A close-up view of the 4.5-inch rockets being loaded into the Seventh Army's jeep rocket launcher.

An M8 armored car troop from the 92nd Cavalry Reconnaissance Squadron (Mechanized), 12th Armored Division, uses an abandoned fortress from the Maginot Line near Guising, France, for a bivouac on 13 December. Half-tracks, like the M3A1 here, were used in the squadron's maintenance and supply sections.

An M18 76mm Hellcat gun motor carriage of Company B, 827th Tank Destroyer Battalion (Colored), near Sarrebourg, France, on 13 December. This unit had used towed 3-inch guns but converted to M18's in late July 1944; it was committed to action in Europe in November. This gives a very good view of the typical stowage patterns of the crew and vehicle stores.

A good study of an M18 76mm gun motor carriage of Company B, 827th Tank Destroyer Battalion (Colored), in Sarrebourg, France, on 1 December. This was a segregated unit with African-American troops and white officers. This unit later fought during the battle for Hatten-Rittershoffen in January 1945.

One of the main drawbacks of the use of the M20 as a command car was the cramped conditions in the rear bay and its exposure to the elements. Some units fabricated their own canvas covers to make the M20 more functional in winter conditions. These are a group of M20's of the 827th Tank Destroyer Battalion in Sarrebourg on 16 December.

An M10 3-inch gun motor carriage of the 813th Tank Destroyer Battalion supports riflemen of the 313rd Infantry, 79th Division, during the attacks toward Oberhoffen on 8 December.

An M15 combination gun motor carriage of Battery C, 106th Anti-Aircraft Battalion, takes up position near a Maginot Line bunker near Lembach on 13 December.

A scene repeated in many Alsatian towns in the autumn and early winter of 1944–45. A series of road obstructions consisting of two vertical log walls with the center filled with earth and rocks have been erected to block major thoroughfares. Such obstacles were usually built by impressing local civilians and were part of the Germans' massive *West-Stellung* fortification program. Here, an M10 3-inch gun motor carriage of the 645th Tank Destroyer Battalion is supporting 45th Division actions near Lembach on 14 December during the attempts to penetrate the Low Vosges.

An M4A3 (named *Buckland Beauty*) of Company B, 23rd Tank Battalion, 12th Armored Division, is recovered by a pair of M32 tank-recovery vehicles after having slipped down into a muddy crater near Guising, France, on 15 December.

An M4A3 of the 23rd Tank Battalion, 12th Armored Division, knocked out by six antitank-gun hits near Guising on 15 December.

An M4A3 (76mm) tank of Company B, 29th Tank Battalion, 14th Armored Division, advances into Wissembourg in Alsace on 16 December.

A column of M4A1 tanks of the 191st Tank Battalion advances through Lauterbourg during the fighting there on 16 December by the 79th Division.

The crew of a 57mm gun of the 77th Infantry's Regimental antitank company had camouflaged their gun on the outskirts of a cemetery near Sierthal, France, on 17 December. Although this gun had become increasingly ineffective in tank fighting, it remained the primary infantry antitank gun through the end of the war.

Although this appears to be an M16 machine-gun motor carriage on first glance, it is in fact a field-expedient Patterson conversion on an M2 half-track antiaircraft vehicle. This vehicle from the 443rd Anti-Aircraft Artillery Automatic-Weapons Battalion (Mobile) is covering the canal near Seareinsming in Alsace on 18 December in support of the nearby 35th Infantry Division.

An M4A3 (76mm) supports infantry from the 68th Armored Infantry Battalion, 14th Armored Division, during operations near Oberotterbach on 18 December. The M4A3 is unusual in several respects, such as its multitone camouflage scheme and the use of a second radio aerial mounted in place of the front-turret smoke mortar.

The wreckage of a German Sd.Kfz. 251/21 is seen near Keintzheim on 20 December. It was knocked out by the French 5e DB during the fighting for the town on 17–18 December. It carries the markings of Panzer Brigade 106. This photo clearly shows the triple automatic cannon mount that distinguished this version of the half-track.

A close-up view of the knocked-out half-track of Panzer Brigade 106. The Sd.Kfz. 251/21 had a triple 15mm MG151 machine-gun mount, which was a dual-use weapon intended both for air defense as and ground fire support.

As the Seventh Army approached the Wiseembourg gap, it encountered one of the most heavily fortified areas of Europe with the Maginot Line on the French side of the border and the Siegfried Line on the German side. Here, troops of the 71st Infantry, 44th Division, look over portions of the Simershoff fortress, part of the Maginot defenses, on 20 December.

An M7 105mm howitzer motor carriage of the French 2e DB conducts a fire mission while emplaced near Erstein on the Franco-German border on 24 December. The ground nearby is littered with spent casings and fiberboard packing tubes.

An M4A3 (76mm) in the streets of Bennwihr during the fighting toward the Wissembourg gap on 27 December. A few days later, the Germans would strike this area during Operation Nordwind.

An M19 tank transporter of the 44th Ordnance Battallion recovers a damaged M4A1 medium tank in Hagenau on 28 December.

An M4 tank (named *Pornoue*) from CC5 of the French 5e DB in the ruins of Kientzheim on 20 December after three days of hard fighting with Panzer Brigade 106. Many of the tanks of the division were whitewashed in the ensuing days during a lull in the battle.

CHAPTER 11

The Battle of the Bulge Begins

THE BATTLE OF THE BULGE was the last major offensive by the German army in the West in World War II. For Hitler, it was a last, desperate gamble to reverse the inevitable tide of Allied victory. Because of its operational scheme, the offensive was heavily dependent on the success or failure of the vaunted panzer force. After Montgomery's British-Canadian 21st Army Group cleared the Scheldt estuary in November 1944, the port of Antwerp was open for Allied shipping. This substantially improved Allied logistics and paved the way for renewed offensives into German in early 1945. Hitler's plan was for a rapid panzer thrust to seize Antwerp and cut off the 21st Army Group from Bradley's 12th Army Group, perhaps precipitating another Dunkirk. In view of weakness of the German army at this stage of the war, such a plan was wildly fanciful and unrealistic.

The focus of the attack was the Sixth Panzer Army, which would attack toward the Elsenborn ridge and then press on to Antwerp. This army contained the majority of the panzer force, including two entire SS panzer corps. On its left was the Fifth Panzer Army with the rest of the panzer force, including the regular-army panzer divisions. The Seventh Army on the far left near Luxembourg was primarily an infantry force and had less substantial objectives.

For his attack, Hitler chose a sector of the Ardennes dubbed "the Ghost Front" by the U.S. Army because of its inactivity. It was manned by four American infantry divisions—two newly arrived green divisions and two other divisions battered in the Hürtgen Forest and recuperating in the Ardennes. The U.S. tank force in the sector was very weak at the start of the campaign, consisting of scattered tank and tank destroyer battalions.

The surprise attack began on 16 December 1944. The initial attacks by the Sixth Panzer Army proceeded poorly, and the infantry failed to make much purchase into American defenses. In desperation, the panzer exploitation force was committed prematurely instead of waiting until the infantry had secured a breakthrough. As a result, the 12th SS Panzer Division became entangled in a brutal series of close-range battles at Krinkelt-Rocherath and then Dom Butgenbach without securing a breakthrough. To its left, the 1st SS Panzer Division launched its main force, Kampfgruppe Peiper, which pushed through a very weak American cavalry screen into the Losheim gap. Initial delays proved very costly, and Kampfgruppe Peiper was quickly bottled up around La Gleize as fresh U.S. infantry divisions arrived on the scene. The failure of the Sixth Panzer Army on the northern wing of the German attack doomed the operation within the first week of fighting

The neighboring Fifth Panzer Army used its infantry divisions more successfully and managed to encircle most of the green 106th Division and to overrun the battered 28th Division. This might have opened a major gap in the center, but the injection of two combat commands from the 7th and 9th Armored Divisions blocked the center around St. Vith for several critical days. As a result, the Fifth Panzer Army shifted its focus to the road junction at Bastogne on the southern side of its advance, which was encircled before Christmas. The St. Vith defense finally gave way on 22 December, suddenly opening up the center. Thrown into the fray, the Sixth Panzer Army's reserve panzer corps raced to the road junctions at the base of the Tailles plateau around Manhay and Hotton. Although the sudden spurt in German advances in the days before Christmas seemed to revive the chances of the German attack, the tide had already turned.

The U.S. 12th Army Group had already massed two counterattack forces in the days before Christmas. "Lightning Joe" Collins's VII Corps came crashing in from the northeast with the 2nd and 3rd Armored Divisions as well as several infantry divisions. The 3rd Armored Division spilled off the Tailles plateau and plugged up the road approaches around Manhay and Hotton in a series of brutal tank battles around Christmas that prevented any further German advances in the center sector. The 2nd Armored Division moved to the southwest and struck the panzer spearheads of the Fifth Panzer Army around Christmas just as they were approaching the Meuse River beyond Bastogne. Much of the 2nd Panzer Division was encircled at Celles, and relief efforts by the 9th Panzer Division were crushed.

The second counterattack force was a pair of corps from Patton's Third Army. These cut through the German Seventh Army and approached Bastogne from the southwest, finally breaking through and relieving the city in the days after Christmas. While the Battle of Bulge was not yet over at the end of 1944, the outcome had been decided. The second volume of this series details the elimination of the German bulge during the January 1945 fighting.

This German propaganda photo shows a winter tank attack by Panthers from I./SS Panzer Regiment 9, 9th SS Panzer Division during the Ardennes fighting.

Some of the best-known images to have emerged from the Battle of the Bulge are the views of the King Tiger tanks of schwere SS Panzer Abteilung 501 (501st SS Heavy Tank Battalion), which served with Kampfgruppe Peiper (Battle Group Peiper). Here, the headquarters company is seen driving through Tondorf at the start of the campaign.

Another view of a King Tiger of schwere SS Panzer Abteilung 501 moving through Tondorf. Peiper was not happy to be saddled with these clumsy tanks, and so he stuck them at the tail end of his column. They consumed enormous amounts of fuel and contributed little to the battle.

Some of the most savage fighting of the opening phase of the Ardennes campaign took place near the twin villages of Krinkelt-Rocherath when the 12th SS Panzer Division attempted to secure the northern shoulder of the salient by overwhelming the U.S. 99th Division. This was one of five Panthers of the first company of SS Panzer Regiment 12 which fought their way into Krinkelt around 0730 on 18 December. Four were knocked out by bazooka teams and antitank guns, and this vehicle escaped down the Bullingen road, where it was knocked out by an M10 3-inch gun motor carriage of the 644th Tank Destroyer Battalion around 1100. It had eleven bazooka hits, several 57mm hits, and three 3-inch impacts in the rear.

This panzer crewman is led away from his burning Panther Ausf. G, seen from the other side in the previous photo.

Another photo taken during the savage fighting inside Krinkelt after Panthers of the 12th SS had broken into the town. The nearest of these two Panther Ausf. G's, probably that of SS Hauptsturm-führer (Captain) Kurt Brodel, has been burned out and its barrel ripped off. They were knocked out in the fighting opposite the village church. Although the 12th SS would eventually push the U.S. 99th Division out of the twin villages, they lost so much time doing so that they failed in their mission to reach the Meuse.

This Panther belonged to the reconnaissance platoon of the SS Panzer Regiment 12 headquarters and was knocked out in the outskirts of Krinkelt-Rocherath during the fighting there on 19 December.

Kampfgruppe Peiper was prevented from moving down the road at Wirtzfeld by some M10 3-inch gun motor carriages of the 1st Platoon, Company C, 644th Tank Destroyer Battalion, which knocked out several Pz.Kpfw. IV tanks on 17 December. This was in the 12th SS Panzer Division's sector, and Peiper moved its forces farther westward.

Trucks of the 372nd Field Artillery Battalion, 99th Infantry Division, withdraw through a junction at Wirtzfeld on 17 December as the 12th SS Panzer Division attacks neighboring Rocherath. The crossroads is covered by an M10 from the 644th Tank Destroyer Battalion. M10's from this unit repulsed a probe by Kampfgruppe Peiper that day along a neighboring road.

German panzergrenadiers of the 1st SS Panzer Division move through Honsfeld on 17 December after the town was captured by Kampfgruppe Peiper. To the right is an Sd.Kfz. 251 Ausf. D, the standard German infantry half-track, while to the left is a captured example of its American counterpart, the M3 half-track. The vehicle in the background is a Möbelwagen 37mm antiaircraft vehicle, one of two knocked out during the fighting by an American antitank gun.

A grim reminder of the human cost of bad doctrine and poor equipment. A knocked-out 3-inch gun in Honsfeld overrun by Kampfgruppe Peiper in the predawn hours of 17 December during the start of the Ardennes offensive. Two companies from 612th and 801st Tank Destroyer Battalions were stationed in the town but were quickly overwhelmed. The poor performance of the towed tank-destroyer battalions in the Ardennes was the last straw, and the 12th Army Group began re-equipping them with self-propelled guns as quickly as possible in early 1945.

Panzergrenadiers from the 1st SS Panzer Division rummage through abandoned American equipment in Honsfeld. To the right is a jeep and behind it a 3-inch antitank gun.

The commander of Kampfgruppe Peiper was infuriated by the failure of the 3rd Fallschirmjäger (Paratroop) Division to seize Honsfeld on 17 December and insisted that the regimental commander turn over a battalion of paratroopers to his column. Some of these troops ended up riding on the engine deck of a King Tiger tank commanded by Oberscharführer (Senior Squad Leader) Sowa near Ligneuville on 18 December, as seen here. The King Tigers belonged to schwere SS Panzer Abteilung 501 (501st SS Heavy Tank Battalion), which made up the tail end of Peiper's column.

Another view of the same group of paratroopers on the engine deck of King Tiger No. 222 during operations south of Malmedy on 18 December. The paratrooper to the left is armed with a British Mk. 2 Sten gun. This tank was lost in Stavelot the following day while supporting Kampfgruppe Sandig.

A King Tiger column from schwere SS Panzer Abteilung 501 passes a line of American prisoners with the town of Merlscheid in the background.

A view of the same column from the other direction as a King Tiger of the battalion passes American prisoners while on the way to Lanzerath.

This Pz.Kpfw. IV Ausf. J from the spearhead of Kampfgruppe Peiper was knocked out by U.S. M10 tank destroyers on the road from Büllingen to Wirtzfeld on 17 December.

When Kampfgruppe Peiper reached Ligneuville, one of its Panthers commanded by SS-Untersturmführer (2nd Lieutenant) Arndt Fischer was knocked out by a Sherman, probably from 9th Armored Division, in front of the Hotel des Ardennes. It is still sitting there later in the month after the heavy snowfall around Christmas.

After finally pushing through Krinkelt-Rocherath, the 12th SS Panzer Division became tangled up in fierce fighting with the 1st Infantry Division in Dom Butgenbach on 19 December. This Pz.Kpfw. IV was knocked out inside the farm, possibly by this M36 90mm gun motor carriage of 634th Tank Destroyer Battalion, which was supporting the infantry. This would be the farthest advance of the 12th SS—far short of its goal.

The battle at Dom Butgenbach hinged on the courage of the infantry's 57mm antitank-gun crews to stymie the German panzer attacks. This is a crew of the 1st Battalion, 26th Infantry Regiment, man-handling their gun from its prime mover near Butgenbach on 17 December.

The Jagdpanther was not often encountered by American forces until the Ardennes fighting. This Jagdpanther (No. 134) belonged to schwere Panzer-jäger Abteilung 560 (560th Heavy Tank Destroyer Battalion), which was knocked out while supporting the 12th SS in the costly fighting against the U.S. 26th Infantry Regiment for Dom Butgenbach manor farm in the opening phase of the Battle of the Bulge. This is from the later-production batches with the bolted mantlet.

GIs inspect one of the Jagdpanthers knocked out during the Dom Butgenbach battle. The 12th SS Panzer Division had lost so many tanks in the Krinkelt-Rocherath fighting that the burden of the Dom Butgenbach attack fell on the tank destroyer elements.

A Pz.Kpfw. IV knocked out during the Dom Butgenbach fighting.

Debris litters the road after the 12th SS failed to capture Dom Butgenbach. In the foreground is a Pz.Kpfw. IV tank of the 12th SS Panzer Regiment, behind it is a Jagdpanther of schwere Panzerjäger Abteilung 560, and on the opposite side of the road is a Jagdpanzer IV of SS Panzerjäger Abteilung 12—all knocked out during the fighting.

In one of the most famous scenes from the battle, Unterscharführer (Junior Squad Leader) Ochsner chomping on a cigar on the left and his platoon commander, Oberscharführer (Senior Squad Leader) Persin, to the right discuss directions while at a road sign at the Kaiserbaracke crossroads on Rollbahn E on 18 December. This photo is frequently misidentified as Jochen Peiper, but in fact, it is from the 2nd Company of SS Panzer Aufklärungs Abteilung 1 (1st SS Tank Reconnaissance Battalion), scout elements of Kampfgruppe Knittel.

Persin and Ochsner walk along a column of vehicles from SS Panzer Aufklärungs Abteilung 1 at the Kaiserbaracke crossroads on 18 December. To either side are two Sd.Kfz. 250 half-tracks.

An Sd.Kfz. 234/1 reconnaissance armored car of Kampfgruppe Knittel is seen moving forward with SS paratroops on its rear deck. The deck of the vehicle is covered with pine boughs for camouflage.

A Kübelwagen utility vehicle of the 1st Panzer Division passes a disabled American 3-inch antitank gun of the 820th Tank Destroyer Battalion, knocked out in the fighting for the Losheim gap in the hamlet of Merlscheid on 18 December.

During the fighting on 18 December in the Losheim gap, Kampfgruppe Hansen overwhelmed a column from the 14th Cavalry Group that was moving on the road between Recht and Poteau. This shows two of the M8 armored cars that were abandoned, both from C Troop, 18th Cavalry Squadron.

An SS-Unterstürmführer (second lieutenant) takes a breather with an SS-Rottenführer (corporal) under one of the disabled M8 armored cars of the overrun column near Poteau. The soldier to the right is decorated with the Close-Combat Clasp, the first and second class of the Iron Cross, the Infantry Assault Badge, and a Russian Service Ribbon. This photo was actually taken before all the "action" photos were staged for the benefit of the German combat cameramen.

A pair of German combat cameramen staged many of the photos along the wreckage on the Poteau road, this one of a panzergrenadier alongside a burning M2 half-track. This is the same SS corporal previously seen under the M8 armored car. Little did the German photographers know that their four rolls of film would be captured several days later by the U.S. 3rd Armored Division and become some of the most enduring images of the battle.

The busy young SS corporal poses again for the camera, this time alongside a disabled M2A1 half-track.

A panzergrenadier from Kampfgruppe Hansen walks along the column of burning American vehicles on the Poteau-Recht road, including several jeeps and half-tracks.

Two young panzergrenadiers of SS Panzer Grenadier Regiment 1 advance past an abandoned M8 armored car from the 14th Cavalry Group.

The logjam of burning American vehicles on the Poteau road forced this Jagdpanzer IV/70 tank destroyer of SS Panzerjäger Abteilung 1 (1st SS Tank Destroyer Battalion) to move off the road cross-country. This was one of the vehicles assigned to support Kampfgruppe Hansen.

One of the final photos on the four rolls of film captured from the German cameraman was this shot of a pair of 15cm SiG 33/1 Sd.Kfz. 138/1 Grille self-propelled howitzers supporting the 1st SS Panzer Division's advance on 18 December. Surprisingly, this type was still in production up to September, and these might very well have been from the final-production batches.

The first of Peiper's King Tigers to be lost was this one (No. 105), commanded by SS-Obersturmführer (1st Lieutenant) Jürgen Wessel, which was abandoned after it got stuck in debris on Rue St. Emilon in Stavelot on 18 December.

As Kampfgruppe Peiper ran out of fuel, it gradually abandoned its tanks. One of the last to be abandoned was King Tiger 204 of the 2nd Company of schwere SS Panzer Abteilung 501, left behind on the road near Gue in the early-morning hours of Christmas Eve after La Gleize had been abandoned. It was later driven a short distance by American troops and is seen broken down along the road near Ruy on 4 January 1945.

Kampfgruppe Peiper left behind some thirty-nine tanks, seventy half-tracks, and thirty other vehicles in La Gleize when they finally abandoned the town on 24 December. An intelligence and reconnaissance platoon from the 82nd Airborne Division later decided to use some of the tanks to test the penetration capabilities of the bazooka on 18 January 1945. To the left is a derelict Panther, while down in the gully is the target of the bazooka team, a King Tiger from schwere SS Panzer Abteilung 501.

The 82nd Airborne Division used a standardized armor kit to reinforce its reconnaissance jeeps, as seen here during the Ardennes fighting.

Kampfgruppe Peiper left Stavelot on its way northwest but was followed later on 18 December by Kampfgruppe Knittel, which fought a losing battle for the town against the 30th Infantry Division later in the day. This Sd.Kfz. 251/9 assault gun was knocked out by a rifle grenade in the fighting. It was probably also hit by a round from the 843rd Tank Destroyer Battalion, as a projectile has passed through both sides of the thin armor plate on either side of the 75mm howitzer.

This Pz.Kpfw. IV was photographed in a holding area in Belgium by the U.S. First Army and is probably from the vehicles abandoned by Kampfgruppe Peiper near La Gleize.

Another view of the same Pz.Kpfw. IV in the U.S. First Army holding area in Belgium.

This Panther Ausf. G belonging to Kampfgruppe Peiper of the 1st SS Panzer Division was recovered from the area near La Gleize and moved to the U.S. First Army headquarters near Spa, Belgium, for a display to the headquarters units.

Another view of the Panther Ausf. G shows its tactical number painted on the turret side; 111 indicates 1st Battalion, 1st Company, 1st Tank.

The principal antitank weapon in the early days of the Ardennes fighting was the 2.36-inch bazooka, which was widely used by the infantry regiments scattered along the front. Its performance was erratic, sometimes quite effective when used by a brave rifleman ambushing a German tank from the side, but just as often useless when fired from the front or from too great a range. Here, an armored infantryman from the 3rd Armored Division guards a road near Manhay later in the month.

A team from the 203rd Engineer Battalion prepares a bazooka near Buisonville, Belgium, late in December. The engineers were frequently assigned combat missions during the Ardennes fighting and were often a thorn in the Germans' side because of their success in destroying key bridges.

On 18 December, these M5A1's of Task Force Harper, 9th Armored Division, were overrun by the 2nd Panzer Division between St. Vith and Bastogne. The wrecks were subsequently used for static defense by the 2nd before being abandoned.

While it is often thought that the Battle of the Bulge was fought in a snow-covered landscape, much of the early fighting took place in cold, rainy weather. Here, paratroopers of the 506th Parachute Infantry Regiment of the 101st Airborne Division march along the Bastogne-Hauflige road on 19 December to reinforce Team Desobry north of the encircled city. In the background are an assortment of armored vehicles, including an M3A1 half-track and an M7 105mm howitzer motor carriage.

Another view of the paratroopers of the 506th PIR of the 101st Airborne along the Bastogne-Hauflige road on 19 December. In the lead here is a bazooka team, and in the background is an M3A1 half-track.

A column of M36 90mm gun motor carriages move forward in support of the 82nd Airborne Division's attempt to halt the advance of Kampfgruppe Peiper near Werbomont, Belgium, on 20 December. They probably belong to the 740th Tank Battalion, a former secret Leaflet tank unit retraining on mine-exploder tanks that month. The unit arrived in Belgium without tanks and scrounged up whatever it could find. At this stage of the war, the M36 was still relatively uncommon, with only 236 actually deployed. Nevertheless, they proved invaluable in the Ardennes, as they were the only U.S. Army vehicle capable of handling the Panther or Tiger. This unit did not come in contact with Peiper that day, as the German column moved east.

Although not the clearest shot, this photo shows a dramatic moment during the Battle of the Bulge as this M7 105mm howitzer motor carriage has been positioned along a road junction leading up to the Elsenborn Ridge on 20 December with the assignment of stopping any approaching German units. The ridge was the key defensive position along the northern salient of the Bulge, and the failure of the Sixth SS Panzer Army to seize the ridge forced the Germans to turn their attention southward toward Bastogne.

Otto Skorzeny's Panzer Brigade 150 was equipped with German equipment modified to resemble American vehicles. The unit was intended to sneak behind American lines to seize key bridges in advance of the main attack, but it failed to launch its intended deep-penetration mission because of road congestion. Instead, on 21 December, they were employed in a conventional attack against the U.S. 30th Division in Malmedy. This was one of their five Panther tanks modified to resemble an M10 tank destroyer, abandoned on the Malmedy-Spa road.

A pair of Panthers of the 1st SS Panzer Division abandoned south of Stavelot after the failure of Kampfgruppe Peiper to breakthrough beyond La Gleize.

This was the Panther (bumper code B-10) of Lieutenant Gerstenschlager, part of Panzergruppe Mandt, Kampfgruppe Z, during the attack on Malmedy on 21 December. With his head outside the turret during the initial attack, Gerstenschlager was fatally wounded by small-arms fire. His crew drove the tank back to the Café du Rocher de Falize, which was the headquarters of Hauptsturmführer (Captain) von Foelkersam, the commander of Kampfgruppe Z. It was the only tank to survive the original morning melee in Malmedy and was disabled in a freak accident in the afternoon during an artillery barrage when it rolled into a wall of the Café de Routier de Falize, embedding the barrel.

A view of Oberfeldwebel (Master Sergeant) Backmann's ersatz M10 (B-7) knocked out near the Café le Maire on 21 December by Lieutenant Snyder with a bazooka hit into the rear engine compartment. This photo was taken sometime after the skirmish with the tank partly covered in snow.

This is the ersatz M10 (B-4) commanded by platoon leader Lieutenant Mandt. It ran over a mine and was abandoned in front of the positions of Company B, 99th "Norwegian" Separate Infantry Battalion, near the Malmedy railroad viaduct. It is seen being removed nearly a month later on 17 January.

This is a rear-view detail of one of the ersatz M10's from a U.S. Army intelligence report prepared after the fighting. It shows the sheet-metal structure added to the hull and turret rear.

This is a front view of the ersatz M10 (B-7) commanded by Backmann of Panzer Kompanie Dreier, Kampfgruppe Z. This tank was knocked out by a bazooka round from an American artillery forward observer, Lieutenant Snyder. Note that between the false bumper codes are the XY markings intended to identify Panzer Brigade 150 to German traffic police.

Although not of the best quality, this photo from the American intelligence report shows the sheet-metal mantlet cover added over the Panther's mantlet in the hopes of creating the false impression of an American M10 tank destroyer.

This detail shot shows the rear-left corner of the turret, with details of the attachment of the false side armor on the ersatz M10.

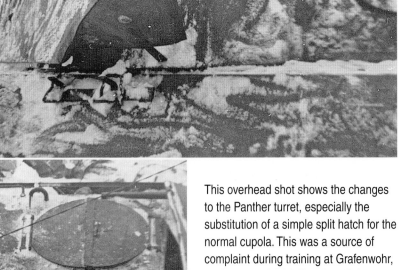

This overhead shot shows the changes to the Panther turret, especially the substitution of a simple split hatch for the normal cupola. This was a source of complaint during training at Grafenwohr, as the crews felt it offered too little protection for the tank commander.

Because of a shortage of captured American equipment, Panzer Brigade 150 used other types of German equipment, simply painted in olive drab with American stars. This Sd.Kfz. 250 was captured by U.S. troops while still on fire.

Besides the Panther tanks, five StuG III assault guns were converted for Panzer Brigade 150. Since they bore no resemblance at all to any American vehicle, their camouflage seems rather odd. The muzzle brake was removed and side skirts added. This one was abandoned near the Baugnez crossroads, site of the infamous Malmedy massacre.

For unknown reasons, a false engine deck was added to the StuG III conversions. In the lower-left corner, the false bumper codes are evident, identifying the vehicle as belonging to the 5th Armored Division, which was not in the Ardennes at the time.

This side view provides a good overview of the changes made to the StuG III for Panzer Brigade 150. Unfortunately, it bears no resemblance at all to any American armored vehicle, in spite of its white stars.

This StuG III of Panzer Brigade 150 was abandoned and booby-trapped following the failed attack on Malmedy. Here, some troops from the 291st Combat Engineer Battalion are attempting to remove the booby traps. Mud has obscured the tactical markings on the vehicle, but the false stars are still plainly evident.

A Panther Ausf. G of the 1st SS Panzer Division knocked out in the fighting near the Baugnez crossroads, where the infamous massacre took place. It has been burned out, but the tactical number 111 is barely evident on the turret side. This is a new-production vehicle with the revised chin mantlet and crew heater.

The threat posed by Kampfgruppe Peiper led to desperate measures. Although the U.S. Army seldom used its 90mm antiaircraft guns for antitank defense like the Germans did with their 88mm guns, the Battle of the Bulge was an exception. Here, a 90mm antiaircraft gun of the 143rd Anti-Aircraft Artillery Battalion has been set up near a destroyed Panther tank in the outskirts of Malmedy on 22 December, supporting the 30th Infantry Division. In the background is the M4 high-speed tractor used to tow the gun. A second battalion, the 110th Anti-Aircraft Artillery, also provided antitank defense at Malmedy.

Another example of a 90mm antiaircraft gun being used in an antitank role to help support the 30th Infantry Division's cordon around Malmedy on 22 December. In this case, it has been positioned behind a makeshift defensive work of sand bags and small timber. The 90mm guns were used on several occasions, including the fighting for Stoumont on 19 December, where they were credited with destroying three Panthers from Kampfgruppe Peiper.

The final German attempt to relieve Peiper by SS Panzer Grenadier Regiment 1 near Petit-Spa on 21 December was frustrated when the leading Jagdpanzer IV/70 collapsed the bridge. Divisional engineers tried to erect a K-Gerat bridge next to it, but it was downed by intense American artillery fire.

The crew of an M10 3-inch gun motor carriage of the 823rd Tank Destroyer Battalion. They were credited with knocking out four German tanks in the initial Ardennes fighting around Stoumont and are seen here on 21 December. This unit was assigned to the 30th Division for most of the war.

A scene in Stoumont after the fighting ended. This 75mm PaK 40 antitank gun had been positioned to cover the N33 roadway. Behind it is an abandoned Panther from the 1st SS Panzer Division.

With the eastern approaches to the Meuse blocked and the I SS Panzer Corps stopped, the II SS Panzer Corps was shifted to the center of the Bulge to support Hasso von Manteuffel's attack. Much of the fighting centered around the town of Manhay, astride one of the more valuable road junctions. This M4A1 medium tank of the 3rd Armored Division was positioned on the N494 road going west from Manhay on 23 December in an attempt to halt the advance of the 2nd SS Panzer Division. It is covered with straw for improvised camouflage.

A pair of M4A3 (76mm) tanks of the 9th Armored Division knocked out during the critical fighting around St. Vith. Two combat commands from the 7th and 9th Armored Division held this critical crossroads, delaying the German exploitation of the penetrations in the Bastogne sector.

Another view of the 3rd Armored Division M4A1 from Task Force Kane along the Manhay road. These roadblocks were eventually overcome by assaults by the 2nd SS, whose 4th Company of SS Panzer Regiment 2 attacked Manhay on 23 December, knocking out several M4 medium tanks of the 7th Armored Division.

A Panther Ausf. G of the 2nd SS knocked out in a fork in the road between Manhay and Grandmenil during the fighting with the 3rd Armored Division on 23 December.

The initial attacks in the center of the Ardennes front had to cross several rivers. This StuG III did not quite make it over the north bank of the Our River near Welchenhausen, which was being defended by the 112th Infantry, 28th Division. The vehicle probably belonged to the 244th Sturmgeschütz Brigade, which was supporting the 560th Volksgrenadier Division in the area.

A portion of the tank-destroyer battalions were equipped with towed 3-inch guns like this weapon covering a road junction in the 7th Armored Division's sector near Vielsalm, Belgium, on 23 December. Although several of these units distinguished themselves in determined stands during the Battle of the Bulge, the lack of mobility and protection of these towed weapons led to widespread criticism in later assessments of the battles.

GIs inspect another of the Panther Ausf. G tanks of the 2nd SS knocked out during the fighting with the 3rd Armored Division in Grandmenil. This photo was taken several days after the battle on 4 January after snow had covered the area.

On Christmas Eve, the 2nd SS Panzer Division swept through Manhay and into Grandmenil, pushing aside Task Force Kane from the 3rd Armored Division. However, after being pummeled by air strikes on 26 December, the town was assaulted by Task Force McGeorge of the 3rd Armored Division and taken in the early-morning hours of the twenty-seventh by paratroopers of the 517th Parachute Infantry. This was one of the 2nd SS Panthers lost in the fighting. It is being inspected by a GI from the 3rd Company, 289th Infantry, 75th Division, which occupied the town on 30 December.

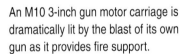

An M10 3-inch gun motor carriage is dramatically lit by the blast of its own gun as it provides fire support.

This particular Panther Ausf. G of the 2nd SS was one of several lost in the fighting at Manhay on the road from Trois Ponts. It is being inspected by American troops in early January after the town was retaken.

An M4 (76mm) of the 2nd Armored Division passes by an abandoned Panther Ausf. G of the 2nd SS Panzer Division lost during the fighting near Grandmenil at the end of December.

An M4 (105mm) assault gun of a headquarters company of the 7th Armored Division waits in hull-down position near Manhay during the fighting with the 2nd SS Panzer Division on 27 December. The tank is positioned in an entrenchment created by divisional engineers.

A well-entrenched M36 90mm gun motor carriage of the 814th Tank Destroyer Battalion holds positions near Manhay on 27 December during the fighting with the 2nd SS.

The crew of an M7 105mm howitzer motor carriage of the 7th Armored Division prepare ammunition while waiting for a fire mission during the fighting near Manhay. The ammunition was packed in the black fiberboard tubes seen here. This M7 is one of the late-production types manufactured in 1944.

The separate tank battalions supporting the American infantry divisions along the Belgian border were equipped mainly with the 75mm Sherman. The 707th Tank Battalion was attached to the embattled 28th Division, and one of its M4A3 tanks can be seen knocked out behind a StuG III assault gun in the village of Clervaux after the fighting. This battalion suffered the heaviest casualties of any of the tank battalions serving in the Ardennes.

Combat Command B, 10th Armored Division, was trapped inside the Bastogne pocket along with the 101st Airborne Division. CCB was divided up into several task forces defending along the southern perimeter of the town. This M4 served with Task Force O'Hara and was knocked out near Mageret.

The Führer-Grenadier-Brigade was committed piecemeal to the fighting near Bastogne, and one of its battle groups attacked the U.S. 80th Division in Heiderscheid on Christmas Eve 1944. It suffered significant losses in the fighting, including the StuG III to the left and two Sd.Kfz. 251 half-tracks. The half-track in the center is one of the rare Sd.Kfz. 251/17's with a turret 2cm autocannon.

A close-up of the Sd.Kfz. 251/17 from the Führer-Grenadier-Brigade knocked out during the skirmish at Heiderscheid on Christmas Eve. The small turret contains a 20mm gun.

The threat posed by the lead elements of Manteuffel's Fifth Panzer Army led Montgomery to deploy the British 29th Armoured Brigade along the Meuse. Lt. Robert Boscawen, commander of 2 Troop of the Coldstream Guards, sits in a Sherman 17-pounder Firefly guarding one of the bridges over the Meuse at Namur on Christmas Day. British armored units were deployed along the Meuse in the days before Christmas to prevent a possible German crossing.

GIs inspect a StuG III assault gun knocked out during the fighting at Heiderscheid.

Another Coldstream Guards Sherman tank on Christmas, talking with the crew of a three-quarter-ton truck assigned to press correspondents. The neighboring 3 Royal Tank Regiment was sent over the Meuse near Dinant before Christmas and stopped the lead elements of the 2nd Panzer Division only five and a half miles from the Meuse in a short engagement on 24 December.

The German Seventh Army forces attacking southwest of Bastogne were almost devoid of tanks at the outset of the campaign. Gradually, more armored strength was shifted to this sector in hopes of securing a breakthrough to the Meuse. On Christmas Day, King Tiger No. 312 of the 3rd Company of schwere SS Panzer Abteilung 501 was abandoned near Engelsdorf. It was later claimed by the 628th Tank Destroyer Battalion. Here, on 8 January 1945, some GIs are using it to string communication wire while a group of Belgian schoolgirls passes by.

A view of some more British Shermans of the 29th Armoured Brigade at Namur, this time with spare Churchill track on the turret for added protection. There is another Firefly in the background.

The Panzer Lehr Division left this Bergepanther recovery vehicle in the town of Morhet southwest of Bastogne in mid-December. This shows the vehicle nearly a month later after the January snowfalls and before it was packed up and shipped back to the United States for evaluation.

The U.S. First Army retrieved a King Tiger (No. 332) of schwere SS Panzer Abteilung 501, part of Kampfgruppe Peiper, which was abandoned near Bourgoument following the fighting in the Ambleve Valley.

A U.S. Army crew from the 463rd Ordnance Evacuation Battalion recovers a King Tiger on board the Culemeyer trailer. This particular tank is the well-known 332 from schwere Panzer Abteilung 501, attached to Kampfgruppe Peiper during the Battle of the Bulge.

The King Tiger on board the trailer with the ramp still in place.

King Tiger 332 was moved from Bourgoument to Spa, near the U.S. First Army headquarters for display to senior staff. It was placed next to an M4A3 (76mm) to show the relative size difference. This tank was subsequently moved to Aberdeen Proving Ground and subsequently to the Patton Museum at Fort Knox.

King Tiger 332 at Spa in January 1945.

King Tiger 332 as taken from a window overhead.

The 1st Company, 504th Parachute Infantry Regiment, 82nd Airborne Division, captured two of these Sd.Kfz. 251/9 assault guns from Kampfgruppe Peiper around La Gleize and put them into use for impromptu armored support after painting them with American stars. This was an assault-gun version of the common Sd.Kfz. 251 armored half-track, armed with a short 75mm gun.

Another view of one of the 82nd Airborne Division's Sd.Kfz. 251/9 assault guns. This vehicle was shipped back to Aberdeen Proving Ground in Maryland for technical evaluation.

Intended to replace the M5A1 light tank, the new M24 light tank began to arrive in small numbers around Christmas. This is from a batch of tanks being prepared at Kornelmünster, Germany, on 26 December and earmarked for cavalry reconnaissance squadrons, but in fact, the first was unofficially acquired by the 740th Tank Battalion and saw its combat debut in the fighting around Malmedy in support of the 82nd Airborne Division.

The catastrophic effects of an ammunition fire and the resultant explosion are all too evident from the shattered hulk of this Pz.Kpfw. IV of Kampfgruppe Maucke, 15th Panzer Grenadier Division, knocked out in the outskirts of Bastogne in late December during a fight with paratroopers from the 101st Airborne Division.

On 20 December, the 116th Panzer Division captured the fuel dump at Samree, but it was pushed out by the U.S. 2nd Armored Division on 10 January. Here, some military police of the U.S. 334th Infantry, 84th Division, try to repair an Sd.Kfz. 250 half-track that had been left behind. The tactical insignia on the bow identifies it as belonging to the 116th's Panzerjäger Abteilung 146 (146th Tank Destroyer Battalion).

This Pz.Kpfw. IV (named *Lustmolch—Happy Salamander* in English) of Kampfgruppe Maucke was knocked out in Champs on the approaches to Bastogne in an encounter with the 502nd Parachute Regiment, 101st Airborne Division, on 26 December.

The approaches to the village of Villers-la-Bonne-Eau, a small village on the southern edge of Bastogne, are littered with the debris of war, including a German 88mm FlaK 36 and an American M4 medium tank, probably from the 10th Armored Division, which fought in this sector.

The farthest penetration by the 116th Panzer Division was Hotton, where hard fighting with the 3rd Armored Division took place on Christmas and the following days. This Panther from Kampfgruppe Bayer was one of a number left behind in the town after the fighting, with a Pz.Kpfw. IV evident in the background. This is a relatively late-production Panther with the crew heater and extended chin mantlet.

A Panther Ausf. G of the 116th Panzer Division during the fighting for Hotton on 26 December, with a Pz.Kpfw. IV (No. 611) in the background. The Panther is a new-production tank built no earlier than October 1944, judging from the crew compartment heater cowling on the rear engine deck. Most of the Panther tanks used in the Ardennes offensive were brand-new vehicles.

A view of one of the Pz.Kpfw. IV tanks of the 116th Panzer Division knocked out during the fighting in Hotton.

Another view of a Panther Ausf. G of the 116th Panzer Division knocked out during the savage fighting for Hotton. Here, a local woman walks past the wreck on 1 January.

A Pz.Kpfw. IV of the 116th Panzer Division knocked out near Hotton.

One of several Panther Ausf. G tanks of the 116th Panzer Division knocked out by the 638th Tank Destroyer Battalion during the bitter fighting for Hotton.

Another Panther Ausf. G of the 116th Panzer Division knocked out in Hotton.

A Panther Ausf. G knocked out by an M18 76mm gun motor carriage of the 638th Tank Destroyer Battalion during the fighting for Hotton.

An M5A1 of the 3rd Armored Division knocked out in Hotton during the fighting with the 116th Panzer Division. By this stage of the war, the prominent tactical markings carried on the hull side have been completely painted over.

Hotton was defended primarily by rear-area units of the U.S. 3rd Armored Division, including headquarters troops. This M4 was one of the two tanks involved in the initial defense and was knocked out during the fighting.

Manteuffel's Fifth Panzer Army made the deepest advance into the Bulge toward the Meuse at Dinant. The narrow finger was attacked from all sides, leading to a series of vicious tank battles for the Celles pocket. This Panther Ausf. G from the Panzer Lehr Division was knocked out during the attacks on Buissonville in the days after Christmas.

The spearhead for Patton's attempt to relieve Bastogne was CCA, 4th Armored Division. The first tank to enter Bastogne was *Cobra King*, an M4A3E2 Jumbo of Company C, 37th Tank Battalion, command by Lt. Charles P. Boggess. It is seen here after its arrival on 26 December.

A close-up of the crew of *Cobra King* in Bastogne after the siege was lifted.

A scene from inside Bastogne after the siege was lifted. The M4A3E2 tank in the center is probably *Cobra King*.

This StuG III assault gun was hidden in a wrecked home on the approaches to Bastogne and held up the 4th Armored Division spearhead until knocked out by 500-pound bombs from strafing P-47 fighter-bombers.

A 4th Armored Division M4 knocked out in the outskirts of Bastogne is recovered by a Dragon Wagon recovery and evacuation vehicle, which consisted of an M26 tractor truck and an M15A1 semitrailer. A close examination of the hull side shows why many crews painted out the white stars on the hull side.

Another view of the tank recovery by a Dragon Wagon outside Bastogne. This was the standard evacuation vehicle in armored divisions in 1944–45.

Lt. Col. Creighton Abrams, commander of the 37th Tank Battalion, points out the name on his M4A3 (76mm) tank to visiting pilots after his battalion spearheaded the Third Army's relief of Bastogne.

The 4th Armored Division spearheaded the Third Army's attack toward Bastogne even though it was seriously depleted in tank strength from its fighting in the Saar region. As a result, it had priority for new replacement equipment, including some of the first of the new M4A3E8 tanks deployed to the ETO. These had the new horizontal volute suspension system, which offered better performance on soft ground than the previous vertical volute suspension.

This M4A3 from the 6th Armored Division was knocked out in Hompre on the outskirts of Bastogne during the attempts to relieve the city in late December. The GI is pointing to where a large-caliber antitank-gun round penetrated the base of the turret.

An M4A3 (76mm) medium tank passes through the ruins of Benwihr, Belgium, on 27 December.

Another Panther Ausf. G of the 9th Panzer Division is inspected by GIs of the 83rd Division the day after the battle there. The 9th lost sixteen Panthers during the Battle of the Bulge, about a third of its strength.

While the British 29th Armoured Brigade blocked to road to the Meuse, the 2nd Armored Division attacked the exposed flank of the 2nd Panzer Division with full force. Here, some M4A1's (76mm) carry infantry of the 291st Regiment, 75th Infantry Division, into an assault near Frandeux on 27 December. The 2nd Armored Division's attacks around Celles shattered Manteuffel's spearhead near the Meuse.

An M5A1 light tank from Company D, 37th Tank Battalion, 4th Armored Division, leads a column of trucks into Bastogne on 27 December during Patton's drive to relieve the town.

This old veteran, a Sd.Kfz. 233 schwere Panzerspähwagen (75mm), was lost in the Celles pocket in late December in fighting with the U.S. 2nd Armored Division. The trident insignia on the bow identifies it as belonging to the 2nd Panzer Division This particular family of 8-by-8 armored cars had largely been superseded by 1944 by the newer Sd.Kfz. 234 series, but some old veterans like this one continued to serve until lost in combat.

Another view of a collection of equipment captured in the Celles pocket. In the foreground is a pair of 150mm SiG infantry guns, and behind them is an Sd.Kfz. 234 Puma armored car.

A view of Celles booty taken from farther down the row shows an Sd.Kfz. 233 schwere Panzerspähwagen armored car in the foreground.

German prisoners walk past an M3A1 half-track of the U.S. 4th Armored Division on 27 December during the attempts by Patton's Third Army to relieve Bastogne. There was intense fighting along the route for the next several days as the Germans tried to sever the link between Bastogne and the Third Army.

With CCR trapped in Bastogne, CCA of the 9th Armored Division was attached to the 4th Armored Division to take part in the operations to relieve Bastogne. An M4A3 (76mm) of Company C, 19th Tank Battalion, Task Force Collins, moves forward on 27 December as part of the effort to open the road from Neufchateau to Bastogne. The tank is fitted with a standardized engineer camouflage kit with Sommerfield matting, a type of metal fencing designed to permit the crew to attach branches and foliage for camouflage. This company seized the town of Sibret from the 5th Fallschirmjäger (Paratroop) Division that day, capturing about forty prisoners.

A Pz.Kpfw. IV knocked out in the fighting near Bastogne and photographed the following summer. It has suffered a catastrophic failure of the front armor, probably a direct hit by an artillery round.

A Jagdpanzer IV knocked out on the outskirts of Bastogne after Christmas.

A Panther Ausf. G knocked out and burned in the Bastogne area. There are at least two bazooka impacts on the turret side.

Snow fell around Bastogne later in the month, as seen here in a view of an M16 machine-gun motor carriage from the 488th Anti-Aircraft Artillery Battalion of Patton's Third Army, which had already broken through to the encircled city. Here, the half-track crew watches as C-47 transports fly supplies into Bastogne on 27 December.

During the Ardennes battle, the Luftwaffe made one last major attempt to attack Allied forces, and antiaircraft units were put on heightened alert. This is an M15A1 of Battery D, 467th Anti-Aircraft Artillery Battalion, guarding one of the Meuse River bridges in Sedan, France, on 27 December.

Lacking paint, some units trapped in Bastogne tried other methods of snow camouflage. This is an M3A1 half-track of the 10th Armored Division using white sheets.

The 5th Fallschirmjäger Division captured six M4 tanks intact in Wiltz and put them back into service after painting them prominently with German crosses. This one is seen abandoned a few weeks later in the center of Esch-sur-Sûre.

An M3A1 half-track from the 4th Armored Division moves forward through Chaumont in Luxembourg during the attacks to relieve Bastogne. The new folding rear stowage racks have been modified to permit stowage across the whole rear of the vehicle.

An M3A1 half-track from the 4th Armored Division passes by a mined jeep from the 25th Cavalry Squadron on the road through Chaumont.

A Panther Ausf. G knocked out by an M18 76mm gun motor carriage of the 704th Tank Destroyer Battalion, 4th Armored Division, during the fighting in the Ardennes in December.

A StuG III Ausf. G with the improved *Saukopf* mantlet lost during the fighting near Bastogne.

A StuG III Ausf. G abandoned near Bastogne.

One of the alternative forms of protective skirts for the Pz.Kpfw. IV was the wire-mesh shields sometimes nicknamed Thoma shields. Although these are often described as antibazooka shields, they were in fact adopted by the German army as protection against Soviet antitank rifles that could otherwise penetrate the thinner side armor of German tanks.

Another example of a knocked-out Pz.Kpfw. IV with the Thoma protective skirts from the 3rd Company, Panzer Regiment 33, 9th Panzer Division, outside Bastogne after Christmas.

This provides a third example of the late Pz.Kpfw. IV with the Thoma shields, this time from SS Panzer Regiment 1, knocked out in the fighting around Lutrebois.

An M4A3E2 assault tank leads a counterattack in the Bastogne area in late December. It is fitted with multilayer appliqué armor on the glacis plate, typical of that added in to U.S. Ninth Army tank units and made from layers of spare track and sand bags and topped by camouflage net.

A 3-inch antitank gun lies wrecked at a crossroads outside Humain after it was put out of action by a German tank a few days after Christmas. This particular gun was credited with knocking out fifteen German tanks during the intense fighting against the 9th Panzer Division around Humain.

Three Panther Ausf. G's stand abandoned in a field outside Humain on 28 December. The 9th Panzer Division attempted to defend the town against an attack by the U.S. 2nd Armored Division but was ejected after a fierce ten-hour battle on the twenty-seventh.

Troops from the U.S. 84th Division inspect a knocked-out Panther Ausf. G in the fields outside Marcouray on 9 January 1945. This was probably one of the tanks from the 116th Panzer Division that took part in the fighting with the 3rd Armored Division in this sector in late December and early January.

A late-production M7 105mm howitzer motor carriage prepares to fire in support of the 101st Airborne Division near Bastogne in late December. The censor has obliterated the unit-identification code on the side of the pulpit.

Preparing an M12 155mm gun motor carriage for action while supporting the 3rd Armored Division around Houfallize in late December.

A pair of tanks of the 3rd Armored Division in the woods near Houfallize. The Sherman to the left is one of the original M4A1 (76mm)'s in use with the division since Operation Cobra; to the right is one of the much-prized M4A3E2 assault tanks.

A GI sweeps for mines near a damaged Sd.Kfz. 250 half-track on the main street of Houfallize.

A Panther tank abandoned in the Houfallize area after the fighting. These overturned tanks usually resulted from American road-clearing operations when bulldozers attempted to shove them off main thoroughfares.

Another example of an overturned Panther in the Houfallize area.

An Sd.Kfz. 250 light half-track abandoned on the streets of Houfallize.

A Pz.Kpfw. III abandoned in Houfallize. This tank type was seldom in frontline use as a battle tank by this stage of the war, but it was still used as a command vehicle in some units.

A scene of the devastation in Houfallize after the fighting, with a Panther tank of the 116th Panzer Division overturned in the Ourthe River near the bridge.

M4A3 (105mm) assault guns from the 750th Tank Battalion fire on German positions from a field near Manhay, Belgium. Like most artillery vehicles, they have been provided with camouflage netting.

A Panther Ausf. A knocked out during the fighting around Bastogne. The tank carries large turret numbers, barely visible on this photo because of weathering; they are of the style more commonly associated with Normandy, so this may very well be a rare survivor of that campaign.

A 105mm Sturmhaubitze assault gun knocked out by the U.S. 99th Division during the Battle of the Bulge. This was a version of the more common StuG III but armed with a 105mm howitzer instead of the usual 75mm gun.

An M4 (105mm) assault gun of the HQ Company, 68th Tank Battalion, 6th Armored Division, moves forward to Bastogne through Habay-la-Neuve on 29 December. The 6th was sent into Bastogne to take part in efforts to break the encirclement on the eastern side of the town in mid-January.

An older M3 half-track (named *Helen*) of a headquarters unit from the 6th Armored Division moves through Habay-la-Neuve during the Ardennes fighting on 29 December. The logs lashed to the side were used to help unditch the vehicle's forward wheels if soft mud was encountered.

Snow began to fall heavily at the end of December. Here, tankers gather around a fire to warm up behind their M4A3 (105mm) howitzer tank near Eupen, Belgium.

An M18 76mm gun motor carriage of the 704th Tank Destroyer Battalion and an M15A1 combination motor carriage half-track from the 4th Armored Division lie knocked out on the southern approaches to Bastogne on 29 December after having been hit by German artillery fire.

An armored infantry unit of the 10th Armored Division uses white cloth for camouflage over their half-tracks while stationed in the outskirts of Bastogne on 29 December.

An M15A1 combination gun motor carriage of Battery D, 197th Anti-Aircraft Artillery Battalion, guards a bridge through the town of Limbourg in Belgium. The bridge is a temporary engineer span built after the original bridge had been destroyed during earlier fighting.

An M36 90mm gun motor carriage of the 628th Tank Destroyer Battalion waits in ambush near the bridge over the Ourthe River in Hotton during the fighting with the 116th Panzer Division on 30 December. The M36 is well concealed under a camouflage net.

The crew of an M5A1 of the 759th Tank Battalion, VII Corps, warms up around a fire at a forward outpost on 30 December. This particular unit was the only tank battalion in the ETO equipped only with light tanks. It served for most of the campaign with the 4th Cavalry Group.

A knocked-out Panther Ausf G. photographed at night.

A U.S. Army heavy wrecker attempts to recover a disabled Panther and Pz.Kpfw. IV of the 2nd Panzer Division in the Bastogne area. Much of the division's armored equipment was lost in the pockets around Celles during the encirclement battles after Christmas.

A U.S. Army Air Force liaison officer poses next to a disabled StuG III assault gun in the Ardennes.

The HQ Company of the 2nd Battalion, 32nd Armored Regiment, 3rd Armored Division, moves forward near Marche, Belgium, on 31 December. The tanks are M4 (105mm) assault guns, while to the right is an M3A1 half-track.

Once the 37th Tank Battalion reached Bastogne, there remained the difficult task of keeping the road open between Patton's Third Army and the town. After Christmas, the remainder of the 4th Armored Division was used to widen the breach. This is a snow-covered M4A3 of the 35th Tank Battalion, 4th Armored Division, operating in the approaches to Bastogne near Sainlex on 31 December.

The crew of an M15A1 combination gun motor carriage of the 777th Anti-Aircraft Artillery Battalion and some paratroopers from the 101st Airborne Division warm their hands over a small fire on the outskirts of Bastogne on 31 December.

The 44th Armored Infantry Battalion, 6th Armored Division, digs in to create defensive positions with the support of an M4 and M4A3E2 assault tank in the outskirts of Bastogne on 31 December.

A turretless M4A1 medium tank with dozer blade is used to help fight fires in the railyard at Ramillies, Belgium, on 31 December.

Another example of an improvised bulldozer conversion in Belgium in late 1944.

Some of the fifteen Panther tanks littering a field between Grandmenil and Houfallize during the fighting late in December.

GIs inspect King Tiger 03 from the headquarters section of schwere Panzer Abteilung 506 (506th Heavy Tank Battalion), abandoned by the roadside in Villers la Bonne Eau on the Bastogne-Houfallize road. The battalion was involved in an attack on New Year's Eve.

Armored vehicles litter the main road through Noville in the Bastogne area after the heavy fighting there at the end of December. In the left foreground is an abandoned StuG III assault gun while above it is a burned-out M4 medium tank. To the right is a destroyed M2A1 half-track.

A StuG III knocked out in the streets of Noville during the fighting in the Bastogne sector after Christmas.

The intelligence and reconnaissance platoon of the 60th Infantry, 9th Infantry Division, developed its own improvised bazooka launcher for its armored scout jeeps, as seen here during the Battle of the Bulge.

Another view of the 60th Infantry's bazooka jeep. The bazookas were mounted on a pedestal instead of the usual .50-caliber heavy machine gun.

Index